SCIENCE
HORIZONS

Silver Burdett & Ginn

MORRISTOWN, NJ ■ NEEDHAM, MA

Atlanta, GA ■ Cincinnati, OH ■ Dallas, TX ■ Deerfield, IL ■ Menlo Park, CA

SCIENCE
HORIZONS

George G. Mallinson
Distinguished Professor
of Science Education
Western Michigan University

Jacqueline B. Mallinson
Associate Professor of Science
Western Michigan University

Linda Froschauer
Science Senior Teacher
Central Middle School
Greenwich, CT

James A. Harris
Principal, D.C. Everest
Area School District
Schofield, Wisconsin

Melanie C. Lewis
Professor, Department of Biology
Southwest Texas State University
San Marcos, Texas

Catherine Valentino
Former Director of Instruction
North Kingstown School Department
North Kingstown, Rhode Island

Dedicated with love
to our colleague, teacher, and friend
Denny McMains
whose talent and courage were
the inspiration for Science Horizons

Acknowledgments appear on pages 316–318, which constitute an extension of this copyright page.

ISBN 0-382-17253-1

Dear Boys and Girls,

This is a special book.

It is about your world.

It is about science.

Science is a way to ask questions.

It is a way to find answers.

You use science every day.

What will you do in science?

You will learn to think.

You will grow plants.

You will care for animals.

You will even meet a giraffe named Daisy.

What else will you do?

You will have fun.

Turn the pages to find out how.

Your friends,
The Authors

Contents

Unit 1
Life Science

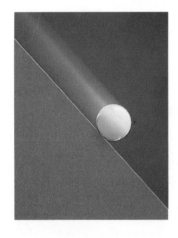

Unit 2
Physical Science

Unit 3
Earth Science

Unit 4
Human Body

Taking Care of Daisy

Would you like to have a giraffe?

This woman has one.

The woman is Betty Leslie-Melville.

She lives in Africa.

Giraffes live in Africa too.

They are in danger.

Some people are killing the giraffes.

A friend called Betty and her husband Jock.
He wanted to save the giraffes from being killed.
"Will you take home a baby giraffe?" he asked.
"Yes," said Betty. "We will help."

The giraffe was not easy to catch.
It was not easy to fit her into the van.
The giraffe needed to eat and rest.
Betty and Jock took her to a stable.

Skills

Thinking of things to use

Betty and Jock wanted to catch a giraffe.

They had to think of things to use.

Thinking of things to use is a skill.

In science you will use skills.

You will ask questions.

You will look for answers.

Practice

1. Think of ways to catch a giraffe without hurting it.
2. Think of things you would use.

3. Make a list.
4. Where would you find the things?

Apply

You want to move a giraffe to a safe place.

Think of things you would use.

Where would you find the things?

"We will call you Daisy," said Betty.

Jock held out a pan of milk.

But Daisy would not eat.

She would die without food.

Finally Daisy dipped her nose in the milk.

Then she took a big drink.

Betty and Jock were so happy.

They hugged Daisy.

Milk splashed everywhere.

Daisy sucked milk from Betty's fingers.

"We need a better way to feed you," said Betty.

Problem Solving

Don't Cry Over Spilled Milk

What is problem solving?

It is finding answers to questions.

You can solve problems.

There are four things to do.

Think

Plan

Do

Share

Betty and Jock had a problem.

They had to find a way to feed Daisy.

Try to solve this problem.

How would you feed a baby giraffe?

Think   What clues can you find in the story?
How do people feed their babies?

Plan   What would your feeder look like?
What things do you need?

Do   Get the things you need.
Make the feeder.

Share   Show your feeder and tell about it.

Now Daisy needed a home of her own.

A pen is a kind of home.

Betty and Jock made a pen for Daisy.

They worked together.

Daisy was safe in her pen.

She ate and slept there.

She had an old blanket to rub against.

She got to know Betty and Jock better.

In a few weeks she did not need the pen.

Explore Together

How can you make a giraffe pen?

ACTIVITY

People helped the giraffe.

They worked together.

You will work together.

Everyone will have a job to do.

The **Planner** gets the things you need.

The **Leader** uses the things.

The **Helper** helps the Leader.

The **Writer** draws a picture.

The **Reporter** tells what the group did.

All means everyone helps.

You need

Planner clay · cardboard · sticks · glue · scissors

What to do

All 1. Use clay and cardboard for the bottom.

Leader 2. Use sticks and glue
to make the sides.

Writer 3. Cut out a giraffe picture.
Put it in the pen.

What did you find out?

All 1. Is your pen high enough?

Reporter 2. Tell how you made a giraffe pen.

Betty wanted to help another baby giraffe.

So she brought baby Marlon home.

Daisy and Marlon ate and ate.

They grew bigger each day.

Today Daisy and Marlon are all grown up.

Daisy has a baby of her own.

Skills

Putting things in order

You look at some drawings.

You find which one happened first.

You put the drawings in order.

a

b

c

Practice

1. Look at the drawings of Daisy.

2. Start with the smallest Daisy.

3. Put the drawings in order.

Apply

Look at the plants Daisy eats.

Put them in order by size.

a

b

c

27

Today seven giraffes live with Betty.

Many children come to see them.

The children ask questions and find answers.

They are learning science and having fun.

You will have fun with science too.

Think about the story of Daisy.

What else would you like to know about animals?

What do you think you will learn about science?

SCIENCE HORIZONS

LIFE SCIENCE

29

Chapter 1

Living Things

Do you see a stick with legs?

It is not really a stick.

It is an insect.

It is called a walking stick.

Some animals look like plants.
Others look like the ground.
Some even look like other animals.
Why is it hard to see these animals?

In this chapter you will learn how living things stay alive.

1. What things are living?

Getting Started

These puppies are living things.
What are the puppies doing?

Words to Know

living things

Living things move in many ways.

How do puppies move?

Living things need food.

Puppies get milk from their mother.

▼ Golden retrievers

▲ Border collies

Living things grow.

What does a puppy grow up to be?

Living things have babies.

These puppies are babies.

How will they look when they are grown?

▼Dachshunds

▼German shepherds

▲ Storm clouds

Some things look like living things.

Are clouds and fire alive?

They move.

They seem to grow.

But they are not living things.

▲ Fire

Lesson Review

1. What can living things do?

2. Why do clouds and fire look alive?

Think! Make up a new living thing.

Tell how it eats, moves, and grows.

34

Problem Solving
On the Move

This thing can move.
It can move in many ways.
How many ways can you
make it move?

Is this thing alive?
How can you tell?
Remember what living things can do.

2. How are plants and animals different?

Getting Started

Think of some ways you move. How can you move your body without moving your feet?

Words to Know

move

▲ Owl

📖 Turn to page 106. Read **Deer at the Brook**. Find out what deer do at a brook.

Plants and animals are living things.

They **move**.

But they move in different ways.

Most animals move from place to place.

How is this owl moving?

36

Plants move too.

They do not move from place to place.

They move in other ways.

Flowers open and close.

How can you tell this flower is moving?

Morning glory▲

Plants and animals need food.
But they get food in different ways.
Animals have to find their food.
Most plants make their own food.

▼ Beetle

▲ Primrose

Lesson Review

1. How do plants and animals move?
2. How do plants and animals get food?

Think! Some animals stay in one place.
How do you think they stay alive?

Skills

Putting living things into groups

Some animals have feathers.

Some animals do not.

You can put animals into those two groups.

Practice

1. Look at the animal pictures.
2. Look at how many legs each animal has.
3. Put the animals into groups by how many legs they have.
4. What are the two groups?

▲ Robin   ▲ Dog   ▲ Colt

Apply

Find pictures of some plants.

Put the pictures into groups.

Flamingo ▶

3. What do plants and animals need?

Getting Started

Do you have plants at home?

How do you care for them?

Words to Know

shelter

Plants need light and warmth.

They get light and warmth from the sun.

Plants also need air, soil, and water.

Wildflowers ▼

▲Butterfly

▲Fish

Animals need food and water.

Animals also need air.

A butterfly has air around it.

A fish takes air from the water.

Badger hole ▲

Animals need a safe place to live.
A **shelter** is a safe place to live.
Badgers live in holes in the ground.
What is the shelter for wasps?

Lesson Review

1. What do plants need to live?
2. What do animals need to live?

Think! Why do badgers need
different shelters than wasps?

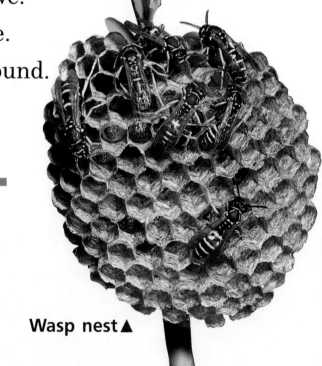

Wasp nest ▲

Explore

ACTIVITY

How can you make a home for snails?

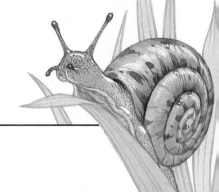

You need

soil · plastic box · water · leaves · twigs · lettuce, carrot, and apple · land snails · plastic wrap

What to do

1. Put soil into the box.
2. Sprinkle water over the soil.
3. Add leaves, twigs, food, and snails.
   Be careful! Wash your hands.
4. Cover the box with plastic wrap.
5. Punch tiny holes in the cover.
6. Watch the snails each day.

What did you find out?

1. What are the snails doing?
2. How did you make a home for snails?

How can people help salmon?

Salmon are a kind of fish.

They used to lay eggs in this creek.

But the creek got too dirty.

These children wanted to help the salmon.

They picked up trash beside the creek.

and Society

STS

They asked other people to clean up the water.
Then the children raised salmon eggs in a tank.
Later they put the baby fish in the clean creek.
The salmon will soon swim out to the ocean.
But some of them will come back.
They will lay their eggs in the clean creek.

Thinking about it

1. Why do fish need clean water to live in?
2. Why do people need clean places to live and work?

Using what you learned

What needs to be cleaned at your school?
Make plans to clean it.

4. How do plants and animals need each other?

Getting Started

Beavers built this dam.
What did they use to build it?

▲ Beaver moving a plant

▲ Beaver lodge

Many animals use plants for shelter.
This beaver cut down part of a plant.
The beaver is building a shelter.
A beaver shelter is called a lodge.

46

▲ Beaver eating a plant

Many animals use plants for food.
What is the beaver eating?

Plants use animals too.

Worms leave droppings in the soil.

They dig tunnels in the soil.

Then the soil is better for plants.

These animals drop seeds.
The seeds may grow into new plants.

Lesson Review

1. How do animals use plants?

2. How do plants use animals?

Think! How does a beaver cut down a tree?

ACTIVITY

Explore Together

How do birds use plants to make nests?

You need

Planner long, dry grass ·

mud · pie pan

What to do

Leader 1. Twist pieces of grass together.
Put the grass into a pie pan.

Helper 2. Cover the grass with mud.

Writer 3. Draw pictures to show how
you made the nest.

What did you find out?

All 1. How is your nest like a real bird nest?

Reporter 2. Tell how to make a bird nest.

Chapter Connections

Think about the ideas in the word map.

Use these ideas to make a puppet show.

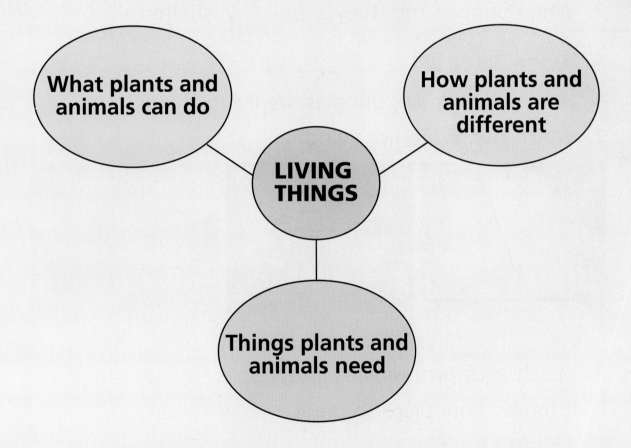

What plants and animals can do

How plants and animals are different

LIVING THINGS

Things plants and animals need

Writing About Science • Persuade

Think of a living thing.

Tell someone why you think it is alive.

Science Words

Match each word with a sentence.

1. A _____ is a safe place to live.   living things

2. Plants and animals are _____.   move

3. When puppies run, they _____.   shelter

Science Ideas

1. How do you know puppies are living things?

2. Which things are not living?

a

b

c

3. Match each picture with a sentence.

   It moves from place to place.

   It makes food.

a   b

4. What do these living things need to stay alive?

5. How do plants and animals need each other?

Applying Science Ideas

Fish need clean water to live in.

How can people keep water clean?

Using Science Skills

Look at the flowers.

Think about how some are the same.

How would you group the flowers?

Chapter 2

Animal Close-ups

What is this woman doing?

She is taking a picture of geese.

What does she see?

The geese have long necks.
They swim with webbed feet.
Feathers cover their bodies.

In this chapter you will learn
how animals use their body parts.

1. How do body parts help animals?

These animals live in the forest.
Their **body parts** help them.
Claws and beaks are body parts of birds.
How is this bird using its body parts?

▼ Bird

—— claws

—— beak

Chipmunks have sharp teeth and claws.

Caterpillars have mouth parts used for eating plants.

They also have many tiny feet.

How are these animals using their body parts?

▲ Chipmunk

Caterpillar ▶

These animals live in the ocean.
Their body parts help them.
Sharks have fins and a tail used for swimming.

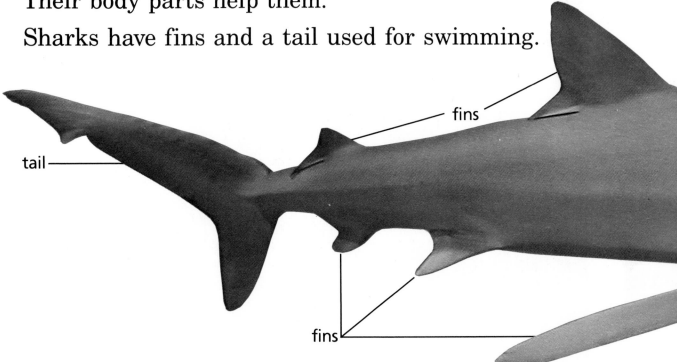

tail

fins

fins

An octopus has eight arms.
Under the arms are little cups.
The octopus holds on to things with its arms.

◄Octopus

▼ Shark

Lobsters have large claws.

How is this lobster using its claws?

◄Lobster

◄ Tortoise

▼ Snake

mouth

These animals live in the desert.
The tortoise uses its mouth to chew plants.
The snake can open its mouth very wide.
These body parts help the animals eat.

Lesson Review

1. How do body parts help forest animals?
2. How do body parts help ocean animals?
3. How do body parts help desert animals?

Think! How does a snake move?

Skills

Getting ideas about things around you

You hear a tapping sound.
You see a bird in a tree.
You have an idea that the
bird is tapping on the tree.

Practice

Some lizards live near plants.
Some lizards live near rocks.
Look at the pictures.
Tell your ideas about where each lizard lives.

Apply

Look at the insect.
Write ideas about how
the insect moves.

2. How do animals move?

Getting Started
Think of animals that fly.
What body parts help them?

▲ Hawk

▼ Bat

Animals move in many ways.
They can fly, climb, or swim.
These animals use wings to fly.
How are their wings alike?
How are their wings different?

▲ Snail

These animals can climb.

Tree frogs have sticky foot pads.

Snails have one slimy foot.

What do koalas use to climb?

▼ Tree frog   ▼ Koala

These animals can swim.
This sea lion has flippers.
How does this turtle swim?

▲ Sea lion

▲ Turtle

Lesson Review

1. Name three ways that animals move.
2. What body parts help animals move?

Think! What ways can you move your body?

Problem Solving

Slow As a Snail

Snails move very slowly.

They like dark, damp places.

They like to eat lettuce and spinach.

How can you get a snail to move?

Think of some safe ways and try them.

Be careful! Wash your hands.

What made your snail move?

3. How do animals eat?

Getting Started

Look at the elephant.

Tell about its trunk.

▲ Bee

▲ Rabbit

Some animals eat plants.

Some animals eat other animals.

Some eat both plants and animals.

These animals eat plants.

What body parts help them?

66

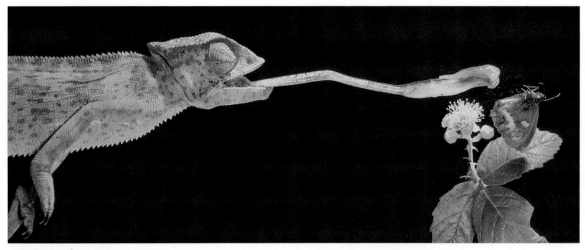

▲ Lizard

These animals eat other animals.
The lizard uses its tongue.
The spider uses mouth parts.
The puffin uses its beak.
What does each animal eat?

▲ Spider

▲ Puffin

Some animals eat both plants and animals.
This bear is eating a fish and a plant.
What body parts help the bear?

▲ Black bear

Lesson Review

1. What do elephants, lizards, and bears eat?

2. What body parts help animals eat?

Think! What kinds of foods do people eat?

Explore

ACTIVITY

How are bird beaks different?

cardinal   heron

You need

2 sticks · 2 clothespins · glue · straw pieces

What to do

1. Glue two sticks to a clothespin.
   Pretend it is a long beak.

2. Get another clothespin.
   Pretend it is a short beak.
3. Pick up a straw with the long beak.
4. Pick up a straw with the short beak.

What did you find out?

Which beak would be better for crushing seeds?

How can people follow animals?

How do people learn about animals?

One way is to follow them.

Why does this moose have a collar?

People put it on the moose.

STS

The collar sends out signals.

A radio picks up the signals.

Then the people can follow the moose.

They learn where the moose goes.

They learn what it needs to live.

Thinking about it

How can people help the animals they follow?

Using what you learned

Tie a bell around your wrist.

Move around the room.

Have some friends close their eyes.

Can they guess where you are?

Can they guess what you are doing?

4. How do people use animals?

Getting Started

List the foods you ate today.

People use animals for food.

People get milk from cows.

This man makes cheese from milk.

What other foods come from milk?

72

People use animals for clothes.
People make sweaters from wool.
Some coats are filled with feathers.
Where do wool and feathers come from?

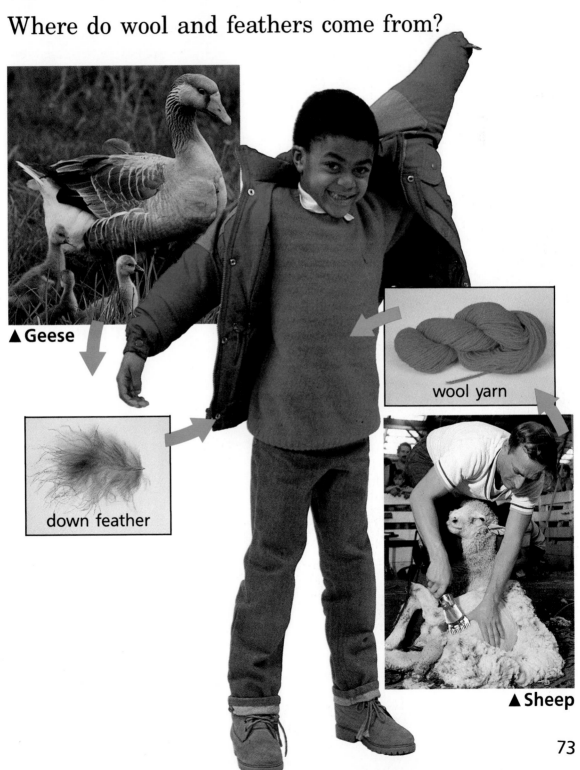

▲ Geese

down feather

wool yarn

▲ Sheep

People enjoy animals.
Many people have pets.
This cat is soft and warm.
How does a pet make you feel?
Some people visit the zoo.
How do you enjoy animals?

▲ Pet cat

▼ Petting zoo

People use animals for work.

This woman cannot see.

How is the dog helping her?

◀Dog guide

Lesson Review

1. How do people use animals for food and clothing?

2. How do people use animals for fun and work?

Think! How do you use animals?

Explore Together

Where does butter come from?

You need

Planner small plastic jar with lid · heavy cream

What to do

Leader **1.** Fill the jar halfway with cream.

Helper **2.** Put the lid tightly on the jar.

Writer **3.** Draw what you see in the jar.

All **4.** Take turns shaking the jar.
Stop after about 10 minutes.

Writer **5.** Draw what you see in the jar now.

What did you find out?

All **1.** What happened to the cream in the jar?

Reporter **2.** Tell the class where butter comes from.

Chapter Connections

Choose one idea from this word map.

Use the idea to make a new word map.

Think of other ideas that go with it.

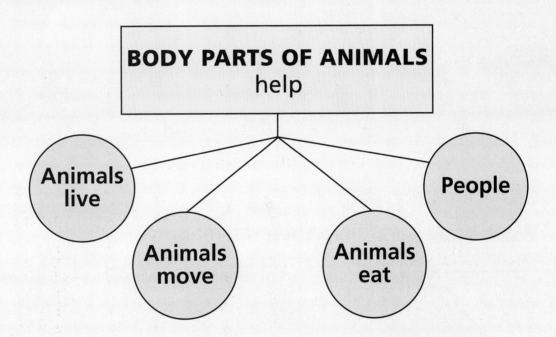

Writing About Science • Create

Invent an animal and draw a picture of it.

Write how it uses its body parts.

Write how it moves and what it eats.

Write how it is used by people.

Science Words

Name each animal.

Tell how it uses its body parts.

a   b   c

Science Ideas

1. What body parts help these animals live?

a   b   c

2. What body part helps a hawk fly?

3. What body part helps elephants eat?

4. How do people use these animals?

a

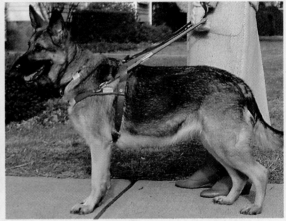

b

Applying Science Ideas

Whales live in the ocean.

How would you follow a whale?

Using Science Skills

Look at the insect.

Write ideas about how the

insect uses its legs.

Chapter 3

Finding Out About Plants

Can you make a picture of flowers?

You could use paint and paper.

But there are other ways to make a picture.

This picture was made with plants.

This is how it looked from a plane.

First the artist plowed a field.

Then he put seeds into the ground.

Green plants grew to make a vase.

Sunflowers grew to make flowers.

What made the dark circles in the flowers?

In this chapter you will learn about plant parts.

You will find out where plants live and how people use them.

1. How can you group plants?

Words to Know

leaves	cones
flowers	stems
seeds	roots

Plants have parts.

You can group plants by their parts.

Leaves are plant parts.

Plants make food in the leaves.

82

All these plants have leaves.

Some have flat leaves.

Some have leaves like needles.

Which leaves would you group together?

Flowers are plant parts.

They are different sizes and colors.

Some flowers have many petals.

Others have just a few petals.

Tell about these flowers.

▼ Bluebells

▼ Asters

▼ Violet

▲ Goldenrod

Seeds are plant parts too.

New plants grow from seeds.

In some plants, seeds form in flowers.

Where are the seeds in a sunflower?

◀ Sunflower

seeds

▲ Seeds

▲Hemlock cones

▼Seeds in cone

▲Spruce cones

In some plants, seeds form in **cones**.
Cones have different shapes and sizes.
Where are the seeds in a cone?

Stems are plant parts.

Water and food move through plant stems.

Some stems are hard.

Other stems are soft.

Which stems would you group together?

◄Birch trees

stem

stem

▲Daisies

stem

◄Pumpkin

▲Bean plant

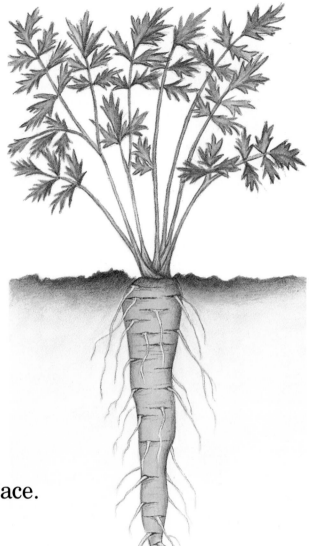

Roots are plant parts.

They help to hold plants in place.

Roots also take in water.

How are these roots different?

▲Carrot plant

Lesson Review

1. Where do plants make food?

2. How do flowers and cones help plants?

3. What do stems do for plants?

4. What do roots do for plants?

Think! What would happen if plants had no leaves?

Problem Solving

Small Wonder

Some seeds are big.

Some seeds are small.

Some seeds do not look like seeds at all.

Look at a bag of small things.

Be careful! Do not put any seeds into your mouth.

How can you find out which things are seeds?

Remember what seeds can do.

Think of a plan.

Then try it.

2. Where do plants live?

Words to Know

forest

desert

pond

▲ Mosses

Some plants live in forests.

This **forest** is shady and wet.

Tall trees grow close together.

Not much sunlight reaches the ground.

▲ Ferns

Ferns and mosses grow in the forest.
They grow best in shady, wet places.
How are these ferns and mosses alike?
How are they different?

Cactus ▶

This **desert** is very dry.

It may not rain for many weeks.

Cactus plants live here.

They must store rainwater.

Cactus plants have thick stems.

They store water in their stems.

▲ Poppies

▲ Cactus

Poppies are small desert plants.

They cannot store water.

So they grow only when it rains.

Cattails ▶

Many plants live in or near this **pond**.

The pond water is still.

Tell about the plants in this pond.

Lesson Review

1. Why do ferns grow well in the forest?

2. How do cactus plants live in the desert?

3. Where do cattails grow?

Think! How often would you water a cactus?

Skills

Learning to read a bar graph

A picture can show what happened.
A bar graph is like a picture.
It can show what happened.

Practice

1. Look at the bar graph.

2. The fern needs watering six times.
The fern needs the most water.

3. Which plant needs the least water?

How Often Do Plants Need Water?

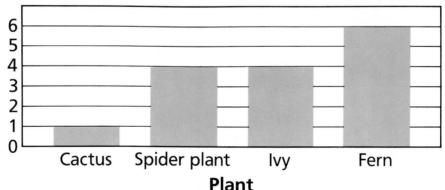

Apply

Which plants need the same amount
of water?

3. How do people use plants?

Getting Started

What is your favorite cereal?

What plant is it made from?

People use plants for food.

Wheat is a plant.

What is made from wheat?

Bananas come from plants.

How do bananas grow?

banana plant

wheat

96

Some clothes are made from plants.

Cotton is a plant.

This shirt is made from cotton.

Trees are plants.

What tree is this table made from?

cotton

oak tree

People use plants for shelter.

Many houses are made of wood.

Wood comes from trees.

Look at each picture.

How are trees made into houses?

People enjoy plants too.

Many people grow flowers and houseplants.

Some people grow vegetables.

How do you enjoy plants?

Lesson Review

1. What do people eat that comes from plants?

2. What do people wear that comes from plants?

3. How do people use plants for shelter?

4. How do people enjoy plants?

Think! List wooden things in your classroom.

Explore

How can you make thread from cotton?

You need

cotton ball · metric ruler · hand lens

What to do

1. Hold a cotton ball in one hand.
2. Pinch a little bit of cotton with the other hand.
3. Pull and twist gently.
4. Use a ruler to see how long your thread is.
5. Look at your thread with a hand lens.

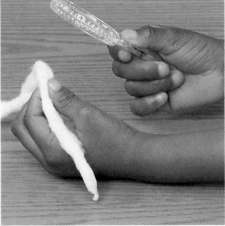

What did you find out?

1. How did the cotton change shape?
2. How long is your thread?

Chapter Connections

Talk about what you learned in this chapter.

Use the word map to help you remember.

Draw a picture of one thing you learned.

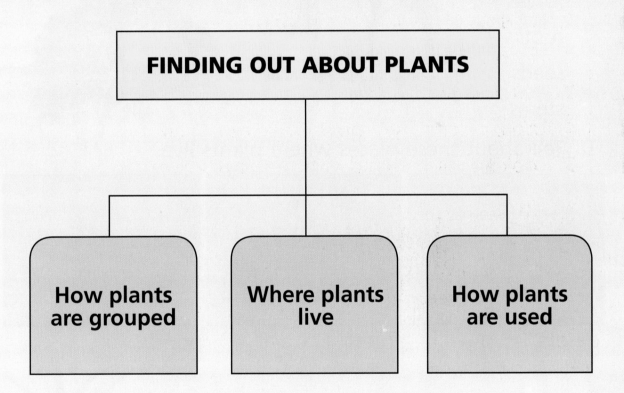

FINDING OUT ABOUT PLANTS

How plants
are grouped

Where plants
live

How plants
are used

Writing About Science • Imagine

Suppose you want to plant a garden for food.

What plants would you choose? Why?

Draw pictures of your garden.

Science Words

A. Match each word with a plant part.

cones

flowers

leaves

roots

seeds

stems

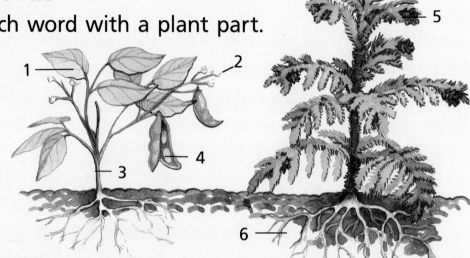

B. Tell about these places where plants live.

desert forest pond

Science Ideas

1. Which plants can you group together?

a b c d

102

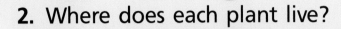

2. Where does each plant live?

a

b

c

3. How are plants used here?

a

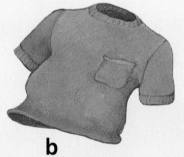
b

c

Applying Science Ideas
Name a plant food you eat.
What plant part is the food?

Using Science Skills
Look at the bar graph.
Which plant is the tallest?
Plant B is the shortest.
How can you tell?

How Tall Are Plants?

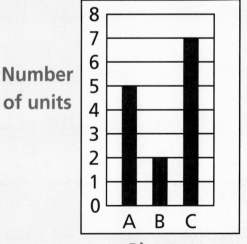

Number of units

Plants

Careers

Animal Doctor

Lynda Ashford-Scales is an **animal doctor**.

Lynda has an animal hospital in Michigan.

She gives shots to cats and dogs.

She gives medicine to rabbits.

She takes care of hurt animals.

Lynda went to school to learn to be an animal doctor.

"I love to help animals," she says.

Connecting Science Ideas

1. Suppose you were a doctor for ocean animals.

   How would you do your work? Careers; Chapter 2

2. Think about the last meal you ate.

   Which foods came from animals?

   Which foods came from plants? Chapter 2; Chapter 3

3. You read about cleaning up a creek.

   List other animal homes people should keep clean.

   Chapter 1; Chapter 2

4. You saw a tiger on pages 30–31.

   Where does it live?

   How does it eat?

   How does it move?

   Chapter 1; Chapter 2

Computer Connection

You can make a pretend animal move.

Learn to move a logo turtle.

Make the turtle hop like a rabbit.

Make it move like a snail.

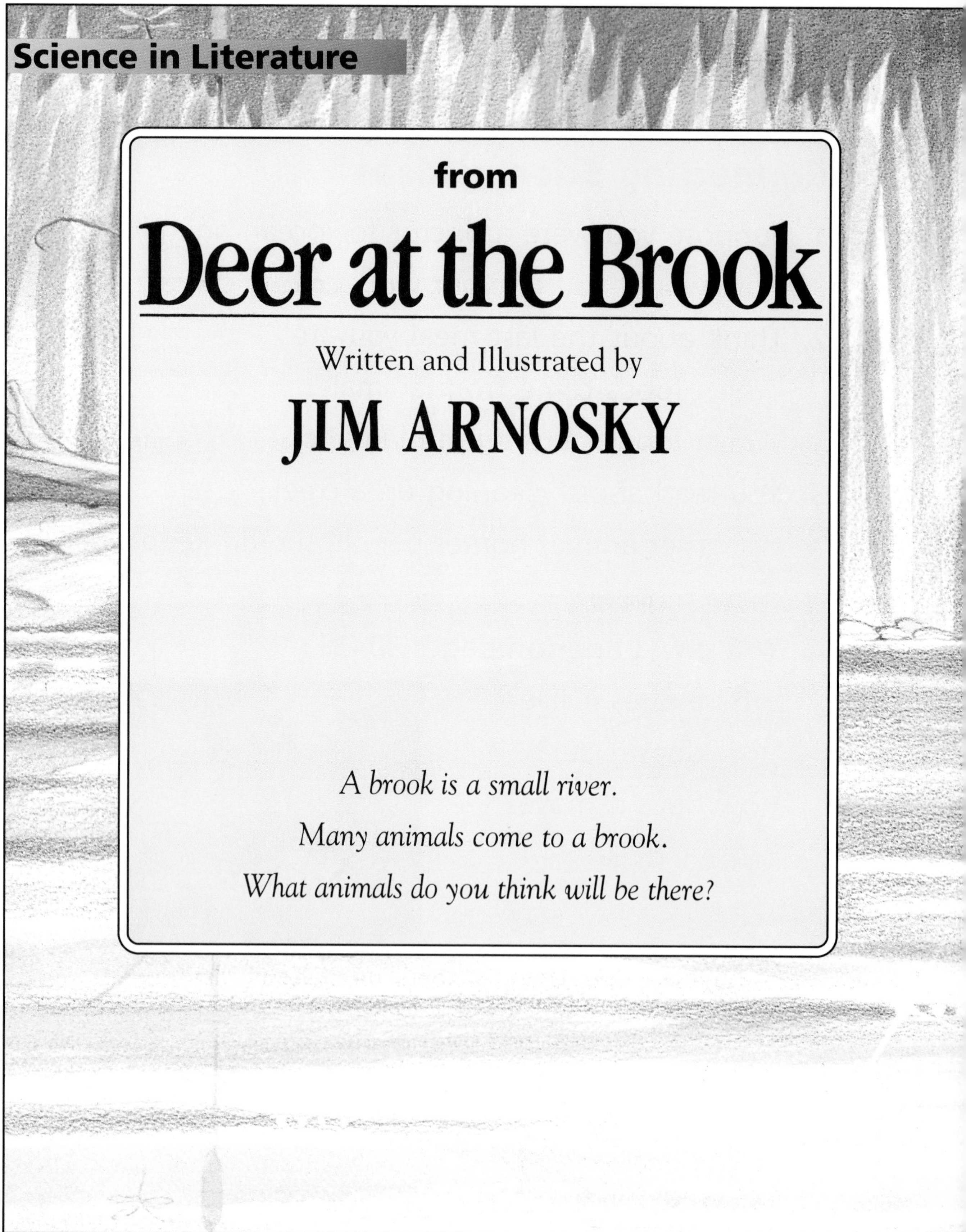

from

Deer at the Brook

Written and Illustrated by

JIM ARNOSKY

A brook is a small river.

Many animals come to a brook.

What animals do you think will be there?

The brook is a sparkling place—
sunlight on water, water on stones.
The brook is a place
deer come to.

Some come alone.
Some come together.
Mothers bring their fawns
to drink . . .
and to eat.

They walk in the water.
They watch the fish leap.

They play on the sandy bank
and nap in the sun.
Sunlight on water, water on stones—
the brook is a sparkling place.

Reader's Response

What would you do if you went to a brook?

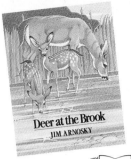

Deer at the Brook

 Responding to Literature

1. What does a deer do at a brook?
   Share your ideas with friends.
2. Where is your favorite place to see animals?
   Tell which animals you see there.
3. Draw a picture of the brook and the
   animals that go there.
   Write the names of the animals on your
   picture.

 Books to Enjoy

Daytime Animals by Joanna Cole
This book tells about small animals.
Some you can see at a zoo.
Some you might see near your home.

Do Not Disturb by Nancy Tafuri
Read about a family camping in the woods.
They do not know it, but they are disturbing
the animals.

SCIENCE HORIZONS

PHYSICAL SCIENCE

Chapter 4

Learning About the World

Do you like to blow bubbles?

This grownup does.

He blows bubbles as large as you.

This man makes chains of bubbles.

How many bubbles are in this bubble chain?

What can you do with bubbles?

In this chapter you will find out how to measure things.

1. How do you learn about things?

Getting Started

Look around the room.

List things you see.

Words to Know

senses

texture

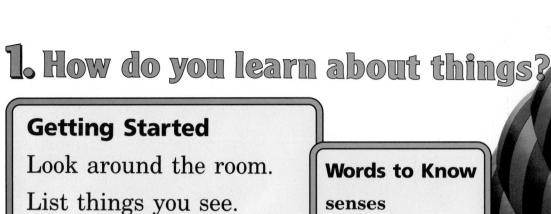

Sesame Place, Langhorne, PA

A fun park is a good place to use your senses.

Seeing, hearing, and smelling are **senses**.

Tasting and touching are senses too.

Your senses help you learn about things.

116

Sesame Place, Langhorne, PA

What colors and shapes do you see?

What sounds would you hear?

What would you smell and taste?

What things would you feel?

Texture is the way something feels.
These close-up pictures show texture.
Tell how these textures might feel.
Are they rough, smooth, hard, or soft?

Lesson Review

1. How do you use your senses to learn?
2. Choose something in your classroom.
   Tell about its color, size, shape, and texture.

Think! Which sense is most important to you? Why?

Explore

ACTIVITY

How many ways can you group things?

You need

many small things ·
4 yarn circles

What to do

1. Use your senses to learn about these things.
   Be careful! Keep things away from your face.
2. Think of a way to group them.
3. Put things that are the same in each yarn circle.
4. Think of another way to group these things.
5. Use yarn circles for your new groups.

What did you find out?

1. Which senses helped you group the things?
2. How many ways did you group the things?

2. How long are things?

Getting Started

Look around you.

Find some long things.

Find some short things.

Words to Know

length

measure

This girl is building a house.

She is using red and blue blocks.

Which block is longer?

How can you tell?

120

Length means how long something is.

The girl wants to know the length of a blue block.

She uses red blocks to **measure**.

How many red blocks are as long as a blue one?

These people caught a fish.

They hold a ruler next to the fish.

They read the number near its mouth.

How long is the fish?

Lesson Review

1. How can you measure length without a ruler?

2. How do you use a ruler to measure length?

Think! What tools do you use to measure length?

THINKING

Skills

Learning to measure length

You want to know how long something is.
You can measure it with a ruler.

Practice

1. Look at the metric ruler.
   It is marked in
   centimeters.
2. Look at a pencil.
   Guess how long it is.
3. Put the pencil next to
   the metric ruler.
   Measure the length of
   the pencil.

Apply

Guess the lengths of some other things.
Then measure them.

3. How heavy are things?

This girl is holding a cat.

She is also holding a kitten.

She can feel which one is heavier.

A **scale** is used to measure weight.
Weight means how heavy something is.

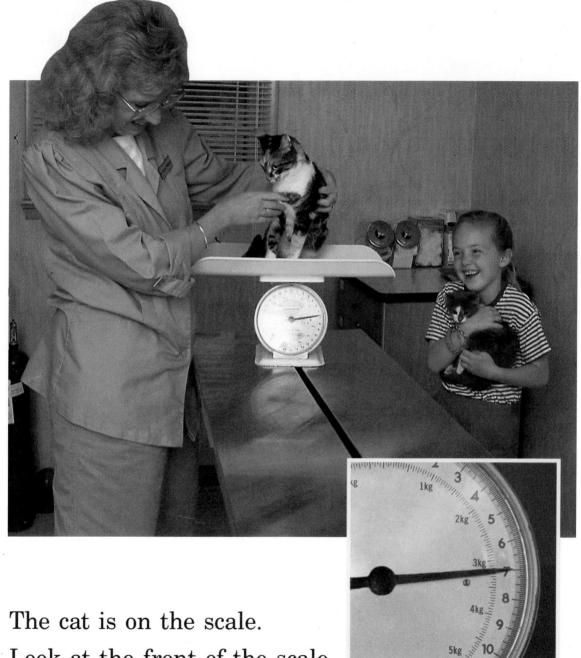

The cat is on the scale.
Look at the front of the scale.
The pointer shows the weight.
How much does the cat weigh?

Many people use scales.

One scale is in a post office.

The weight shows on a screen.

The other scale is in a food store.

The pointer shows the weight.

Lesson Review

1. You have two boxes.

How can you tell which is heavier?

2. How do you use the scale in a food store?

Think! Name something that is small but heavy.

Explore Together

Which thing is the heaviest?

You need

 3 small things · scale

What to do

Leader 1. Pick up each thing.

Guess which is lightest and heaviest.

Be careful! Keep things out of your eyes and mouth.

Writer 2. Draw each thing from lightest to heaviest.

Helper 3. Weigh each thing on the scale.

Writer 4. Write down how much each thing weighs.

Draw each thing from lightest to heaviest.

What did you find out?

All 1. How close were your guesses?

Reporter 2. Which thing is the heaviest?

127

Suppose you are very thirsty.

You want the glass with the most juice.

But these glasses have different shapes.

It is hard to tell which holds the most.

One way to tell is by measuring.

Explore Together
Which thing is the heaviest?

You need

Planner 3 small things · scale

What to do

Leader **1.** Pick up each thing.

Guess which is lightest and heaviest.

Be careful! Keep things out of your eyes and mouth.

Writer **2.** Draw each thing from lightest to heaviest.

Helper **3.** Weigh each thing on the scale.

Writer **4.** Write down how much each thing weighs.

Draw each thing from lightest to heaviest.

What did you find out?

All **1.** How close were your guesses?

Reporter **2.** Which thing is the heaviest?

4. How much do things hold?

Some things hold more than others do.

They have more space inside.

Some things do not hold very much.

They have less space inside.

These boxes are the same shape.

It is easy to tell which box holds more.

One box is bigger than the other.

Which box holds more?

Suppose you are very thirsty.

You want the glass with the most juice.

But these glasses have different shapes.

It is hard to tell which holds the most.

One way to tell is by measuring.

Each glass is empty now.
The juice was poured into three measuring cups.
Which glass held the most juice?

Lesson Review

1. Two boxes are the same shape.
   How can you find out which holds more marbles?
2. How can you measure how much water
   something holds?

Think! How can you measure how much water
a bathtub holds?

Problem Solving

Don't Spill the Beans

Beans, beans, lots of beans.

Where can we put these beans?

Find things that can hold beans.

Which thing can hold the most beans?

How can you find out?

Test your idea.

Chapter Connections

Copy the word map on paper.

Leave out some words.

Trade papers with a classmate.

Write the missing words.

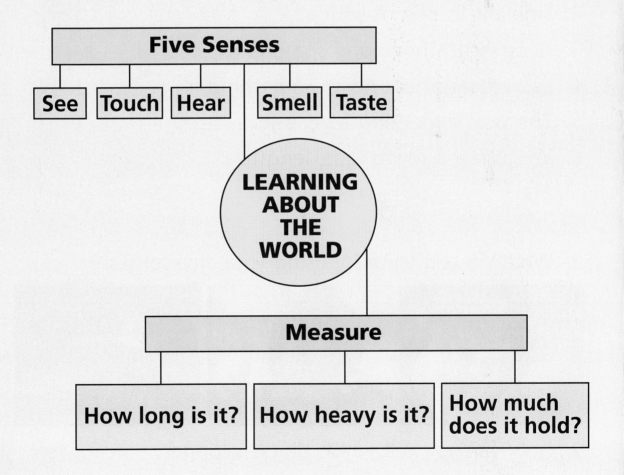

Writing About Science • Research

Use your five senses to tell about a peanut.

Science Words

Fill in each missing word.

length   measure   scale

senses   texture   weight

1. A _____ is used to measure weight.

2. Smelling is one of your _____.

3. _____ means how long something is.

4. _____ means how heavy something is.

5. The way something feels is its _____.

6. You use a ruler to _____ length.

Science Ideas

1. What do you learn by using your five senses?

2. How can you tell which block is longer?

134

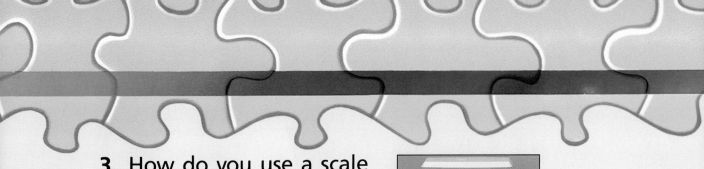

3. How do you use a scale to measure weight?

4. How can you tell which glass holds more juice?

Applying Science Ideas

You see footprints in the mud.

You forgot your ruler.

How can you find the length of the footprints?

Using Science Skills

Guess how long a crayon is.

Then measure the length of the crayon.

Chapter 5

How Things Move

Can paper fly?

It can if you fold it right and throw it.

Some people make paper airplanes.

They hold contests each year.

Some airplanes fly far.

Some stay in the air for a long time.

This simple plane flew for four seconds. The shape of an airplane helps it move. Which airplane would you like to make?

In this chapter you will learn how things move, what makes them move, and how you use moving things.

1. How do things move?

Getting Started

Make a chair move.

How did you do it?

Words to Know

force

Toys are not alive.

But many toys move.

Some toys spin, roll, or bounce.

Tell how these toys move.

138

A moving thing changes place.
The spring toy started on the top step.
Then it moved down to the next step.
How did the yo-yo change places?

▲ Boy pushing

Things cannot start to move by themselves.

Something must push them or pull them.

You move things away from you with a push.

You move things toward you with a pull.

A push or a pull is called a **force**.

▲ Children pulling

A beach ball is very light.

You can start it moving with a small force.

A bowling ball is heavy.

A large force is needed to start it.

This path is smooth.

It takes a small force to skate on this path.

Grass is harder to skate on.

Will a small force move the skates over grass?

▲ Skating on a path

▲ Skating on grass

Lesson Review

1. How do you know that things move?

2. What is a force?

Think! What are five ways you can move?

Skills

Telling what may happen

You watch a toy car roll down a ramp.
You guess how far it will go next time.

Practice

1. Roll a toy car from the top of a ramp.
   Watch how far it goes.
2. Roll the car from the middle of the ramp.
   Watch how far it goes.
3. Think about rolling the car from near the bottom of the ramp.
   Guess how far it will go.

Apply

Think about the toy car on the ramp.
Guess which sled in the picture will go farther.

How do machines walk?

Many machines can move.

Cars and bikes move by rolling on wheels.

Some new machines move by walking on legs.

How do people make walking machines?

They study how insects move.

Then they build machines to move the same way.

Walking machines step over walls and climb hills.

Some walking machines dig in rivers.

They make rivers deeper for big boats.

Walking machines help to move things too.
They make work easier for people.

Thinking about it

What job could a walking machine do
around your school?

Using what you learned

Think about an insect or other animal.
What body parts help it move?
Draw a machine that works like that
animal.
What special things can the machine do?

2. What are some types of forces?

Getting Started

Drop a pencil.
Which way does it go?

Words to Know

gravity

This ball is falling.
A force pulls it to the earth.
The force is called **gravity**.
Gravity pulls everything to the earth.

Magnets have force too.

This force is different from gravity.

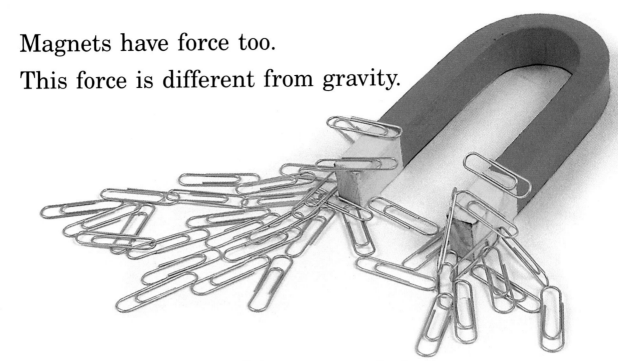

Magnets pull some things toward them.

But they do not pull everything.

They pull only some metals.

What things do these magnets pull?

Some toys have magnets.

The magnets move things or hold things.

Find the magnets in these toys.

How are the magnets used?

Lesson Review

1. What is gravity?

2. What do magnets do?

Think! How do you use magnets?

Explore
What can a magnet pull?

You need

small things ·

chart paper ·

crayons ·

magnet

What to do

1. Guess which things a
   magnet can pull.
2. Make a chart like the one shown.
3. Touch each thing with a magnet.
   Does the magnet pull it?
4. Draw each thing on the chart.

What did you find out?

1. How close were your guesses?
2. Which things does the magnet pull?

3. How do people use machines?

Getting Started

Name something with wheels.

How do the wheels help?

Words to Know

machines   ramp

wheel   lever

People use machines to move things.

Machines make work easier.

They help us push, pull, or lift.

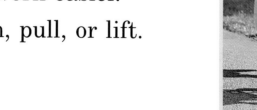

150

A **wheel** is a machine.

A bicycle has wheels.

What other wheels do you see?

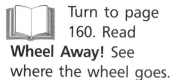

Turn to page 160. Read **Wheel Away!** See where the wheel goes.

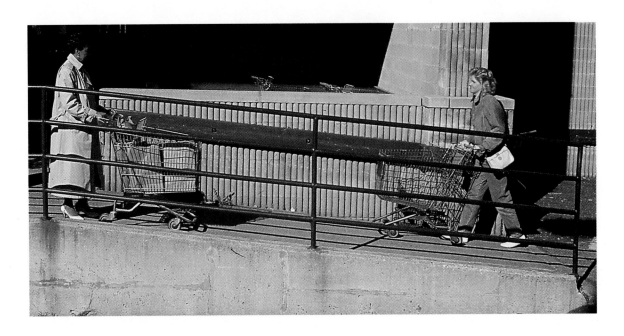

A **ramp** is also a machine.

Ramps make it easier to lift things.

How are these people using ramps?

A **lever** is a machine.

Levers make it easier to lift things.

How are the levers in these pictures used?

lever

lever

Lesson Review

1. Name three kinds of machines.

2. How do people use machines?

Think! Find some machines around your school.

Explore Together

Does a ramp make work easier?

You need

Planner tape · rubber band · plastic mug · metric ruler · ramp

What to do

Helper 1. Tape a rubber band to a mug handle.

Leader 2. Lift the mug with the rubber band.

Writer 3. Measure the length of the rubber band.

Leader 4. Now pull the mug up the ramp.

Writer 5. Measure the rubber band again.

What did you find out?

All 1. When was the rubber band longer?

Reporter 2. Does a ramp make work easier?

154

Chapter Connections

Look at the word map.

List things that move.

Tell what forces make them move.

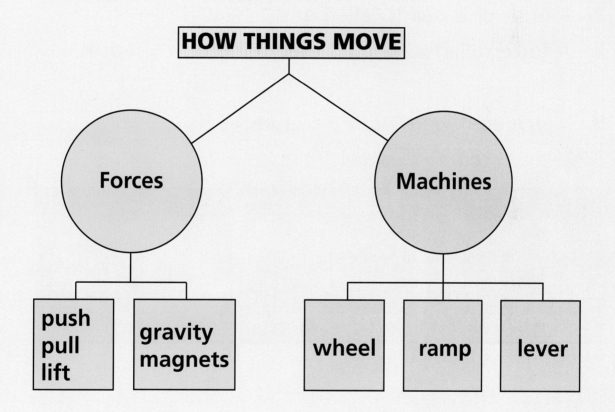

Writing About Science • Describe

Draw a picture of a machine.

Show it moving something.

Tell about the kind of force used.

Science Words

A. Fill in each missing word.

force   gravity   machines

1. You use wheels and other ____ to move things.

2. A push or a pull is called a ____.

3. A force called ____ pulls everything on the earth.

B. Match each word with a picture.

lever   ramp   wheel

a

b

c

Science Ideas

1. How do you know that this toy moved?

2. What will happen when the
boy pushes the merry-go-round?

3. What things do gravity and magnets move?

4. How do people use wheels, ramps, and levers?

Applying Science Ideas

You want to build a machine
that moves in water.
What animal might it look like?

Using Science Skills

Roll a toy car from the top of a low ramp.
Roll the car from the top of a higher ramp.
Guess how far the car will go from an
even higher ramp.

Careers

Toy Maker

Alton Takeyasu liked art in school.

Now he is a **toy maker** in Ohio.

"It is fun to make toys," says Alton.

Alton gets ideas for new toys from books.

He gets ideas from movies too.

Alton makes models of new toys.

Then children try out the toys.

Connecting Science Ideas

1. Think of a toy you like.

What would you tell Alton to make it work better?

Careers; Chapter 5

2. You saw a machine that walks.

How could it be changed to have senses like a person?

Chapter 4; Chapter 5

3. You want to weigh an elephant.

What could you use to move it onto the scale?

Chapter 4; Chapter 5

Unit Project

Make a magnet toy.

Draw a maze on a shoe box.

Put the toy on the maze.

Move it with another magnet.

from

WHEEL AWAY!

Written by **Dayle Ann Dodds**

Illustrated by **Thacher Hurd**

Oh no! See it go!

Oh no! See it go.

Follow the wheel down the hill.

Follow the wheel up the hill.

pa-da-rump

pa-da-rump

pa-da-rump-pump-pump

In the lake

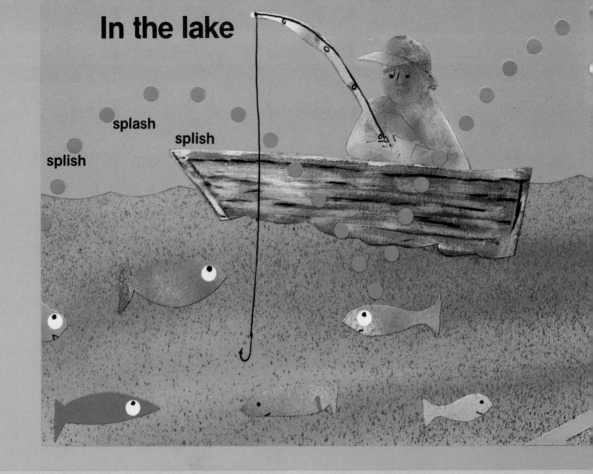

splash

splish

splish

slowing

162

Over the cake

squish

squash

squish

Oh no! See it go!

pa-da-rump   pa-da-rump   pa-da-rump-pump-pump

slowing

slowing

slowing

Oh no!

163

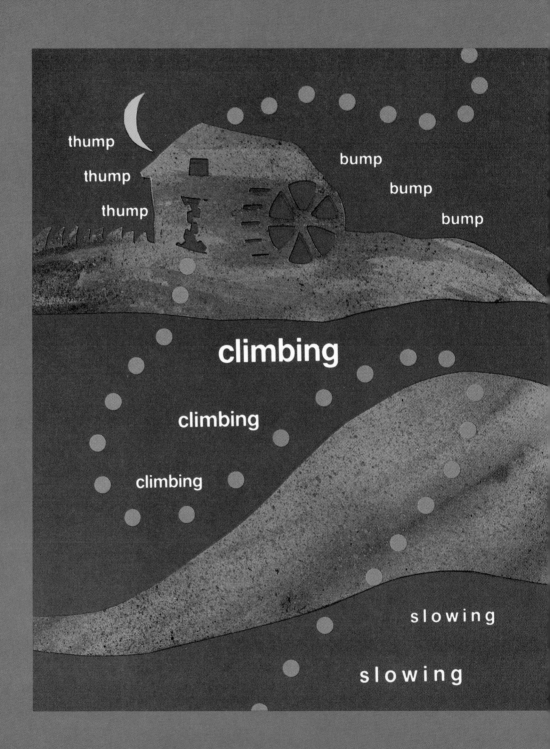

slowing

back.

Reader's Response

Think of other places the wheel could go.

📖 **Responding to Literature**

1. When does the wheel go fast?
   When does it go slow?

2. Draw a picture of the man in the boat.
   Write what he might say when he sees
   the wheel.

3. Bicycles move on wheels.
   Name other things that have wheels.

📖 **Books to Enjoy**

**Monster Trucks and Other Giant
Machines on Wheels** by Jerry Bushey
Look at big machines with wheels.

Machines by Ann and Harlow Rockwell
Do you know how gears and pulleys work?
Learn about these and other machines.

SCIENCE
HORIZONS

EARTH SCIENCE

Looking at the Sky

Twinkle, twinkle, little star,
How I wonder what you are!
Up above the world so high,
Like a diamond in the sky.

Look at the sky above the mountain.
The sky is very dark.
The stars are as bright as diamonds!

Look at the sky above the city.
The sky is not dark there.
The city lights block out the stars.

In this chapter you will learn about the sun, the moon, and the stars.

1. How does the sky change?

Getting Started

Look at a book close up.

Now look at it from far away.

How does it look different?

Words to Know

sunrise

sunset

The sun, moon, and stars are very, very big.

But they look very small from the earth.

Things look smaller from far away.

Name a big thing that looks small from far away.

170

The sky changes during the day.
Each morning the sun is in the east.
This time of day is called **sunrise**.
The sun seems to move across the sky each day.
At noon, the sun appears high in the sky.
Each evening the sun is in the west.
This time of day is called **sunset**.
What happens to the sky after sunset?

▲ Sun low in the sky

▲ Sun high in the sky

Each day the sun lights the sky.

In winter the sky is light for a short time.

It gets dark early.

In summer the sky is light for a long time.

Which picture shows summer?

7:00 pm

7:00 pm

Lesson Review

1. Why does the sun look small?
2. How does the sky change during the day?
3. What time of year is the sky light for a long time?

Think! How does what you do change as the sky changes?

Skills

Reading a data table

A table is a list of words and numbers. A table can help you learn about something.

Practice

Look at the table. It shows that there are 10 hours of daylight in winter. How many hours of daylight are there in summer?

Time of Year	Hours of Daylight
Winter	10
Spring	12
Summer	14
Fall	12

Apply

Which times of year have the same number of daylight hours?

2. How does the moon look?

Getting Started

Look outside at night.

Can you see the moon?

How does it look from the earth?

Words to Know

full moon

The shape of the moon seems to change.

Sometimes the moon looks like a circle.

Sometimes it looks like part of a circle.

Sometimes you do not see the moon at all.

174

Find the moon that looks like a circle.

This is called a **full moon**.

The moon looks biggest at full moon.

You see these changing shapes each month.

▲ Moon in the night sky

The moon has high and low places.

From the earth they look like light and dark spots.

Why do the spots look small from the earth?

Lesson Review

1. How does the moon seem to change its shape?

2. What are the spots you see on the moon?

Think! How is the moon different from the earth?

Explore Together

Why does the moon look small?

You need

big ball · meterstick

What to do

Helper **1.** Hold a ball in front of you.

Leader **2.** Stand 1 meter away. Hold a meterstick near your face to measure the ball.

Writer **3.** Make a chart like this one.

Distance from ball	Size of ball
1 meter	
2 meters	
3 meters	
4 meters	

Leader **4.** Repeat step **2** from farther away.

Writer **5.** Mark the chart at each distance.

What did you find out?

Reporter **1.** What seemed to happen to the ball?

All **2.** Why does the moon look small?

177

3. How do the stars look?

Getting Started

Think about the sky at night.
What might you see?

Words to Know

star

▲Night sky with moon and stars

You can see stars in the night sky.
A **star** is a body in space.
Stars give off light as the sun does.

178

▲Night sky with Big Dipper

Some stars seem to make patterns in the sky.

One star pattern is called the Big Dipper.

What is the shape of the Big Dipper?

Each night the star patterns seem to move a little.

Each season you see different star patterns.

The sun is a star.

Many stars are bigger than the sun.

But those stars are very far away.

So they look smaller than the sun.

How would the sun look from far away in space?

▼ Sun from space

▲ Sun from the earth

Lesson Review

1. How are the stars like the sun?

2. How do star patterns change?

Think! Why can you not see stars in the daytime?

Explore

How can you make a star pattern?

You need

cardboard tube · aluminum foil · rubber band · sharp pencil · flashlight

What to do

1. Put aluminum foil over one end of a cardboard tube.
2. Put a rubber band around the foil.
3. Make holes in the foil with a sharp pencil.
4. Shine a flashlight through the open end of the tube.
5. Look at the pattern.

What did you find out?

1. How is your pattern like a star pattern?
2. Write a story about your pattern.

What went on in the sky last night?

People study the stars.

But people cannot stay up all night.

This telescope can.

It works while you sleep.

It does not need to rest.

It sees things that people might miss.

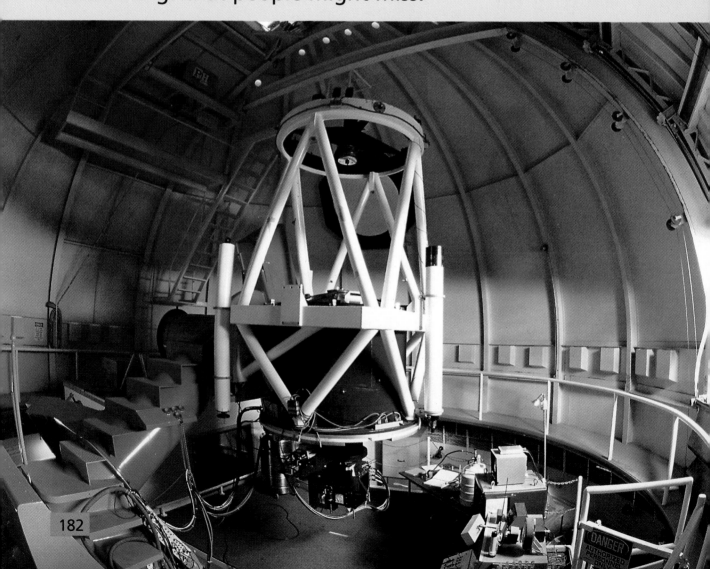

The telescope has help.

A computer works with it.

Each day people check the computer.

It tells them about the stars.

Thinking about it

1. What can telescopes do better than people?

2. Why do people need to check the telescope's computer each day?

Using what you learned

Think of something you do.

Draw a new machine that could help you.

Tell how it works.

4. What time is it?

Getting Started

Is it light or dark outside?

What do you do when it is light?

Words to Know

daytime

night

Part of a day is light, and part is dark.

The light part of a day is called **daytime**.

The dark part of a day is called **night.**

◀Children in school

▼City in daytime

You can tell the time of day in many ways.

The sun is low in the sky in the morning.

It is high in the sky at noon.

How do these pictures show the time?

◀ Family eating dinner

▼ City at night

185

Shadows also show the time of day.

Shadows are long in the morning.

They are shorter at noon.

Shadows are long again in late afternoon.

Which picture shows noon?

A day is 24 hours long.

You use clocks to tell the time of day.

Clocks measure hours and minutes.

A minute is a small part of a day.

What can you do in 1 minute?

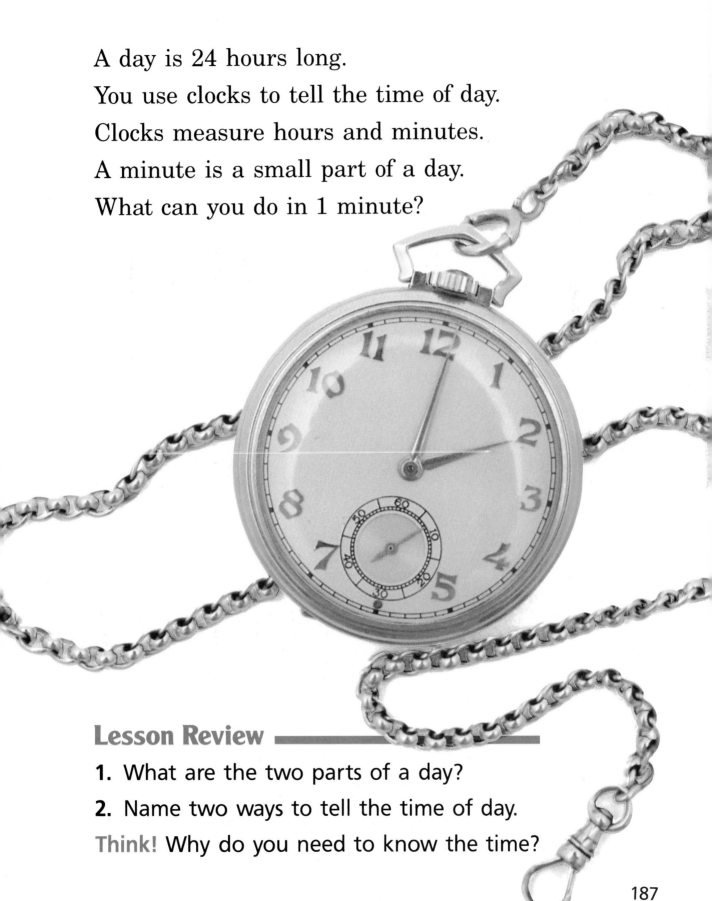

Lesson Review

1. What are the two parts of a day?

2. Name two ways to tell the time of day.

Think! Why do you need to know the time?

Problem Solving
Just Me and My Shadow

Shadows change during the day.
They may become longer or shorter.
They may point one way and
then another.

**How do shadows change
during the day?**
Use chalk to trace your shadow
on the sidewalk.

Think of a plan to see how your shadow changes
during the day. Then try it.

Chapter Connections

Copy the shapes shown in the word map.
Fill in pictures instead of words.

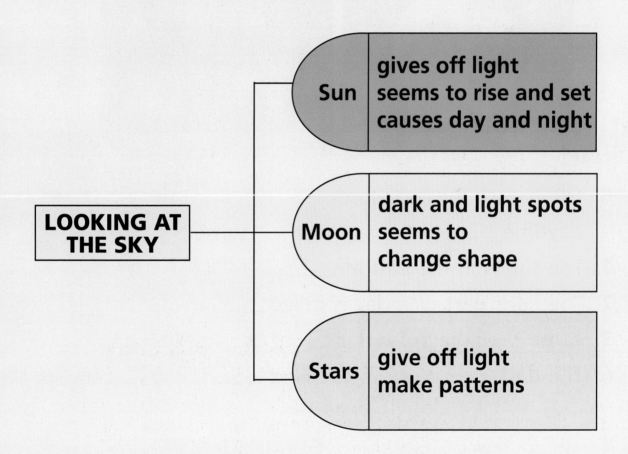

LOOKING AT THE SKY

Sun
gives off light
seems to rise and set
causes day and night

Moon
dark and light spots
seems to
change shape

Stars
give off light
make patterns

Writing About Science • Research

Make a book with five pages.

Draw a picture of the sky for five days or five nights.

Chapter 6 Review

Science Words

A. Match each word with a picture.

full moon   stars

a

b

B. Fill in each missing word.

daytime   night   sunrise   sunset

1. The sun is in the east at ____.

2. The light part of a day is called ____.

3. After ____ the sky is dark.

4. The dark part of a day is called ____.

Science Ideas

1. How does the sky change during the day?

2. What are some shapes of the moon?

3. How do the stars look from the earth?

4. How can you tell what time it is?

Applying Science Ideas

You can watch the stars with a telescope. What other things in the sky could you watch?

Using Science Skills

The table shows the length of a shadow. At what time is the shadow shortest?

Time	Shadow in centimeters
Morning	40
Noon	20
Afternoon	40
Evening	80

Chapter 7

Looking at the Earth

Look at all the hot-air balloons!

Think about going for a ride in one.

What would you see?

In some places you would see lakes.

Other places might have mountains.

Think about your city or town.

You know how it looks from the ground.

How would it look from a balloon?

In this chapter you will learn how the earth looks from the ground, from a jet, and from space.

1. How does the earth look from space?

Getting Started

Look at a penny from far away.

Now look at it close up.

How does it look different?

Words to Know

earth

The **earth** is where you live.

How does the earth look to you?

You know you are on the earth.

But you can see only a small part of it.

You cannot see the whole earth.

▼ Flat land

▲ **Earth from space**

The earth looks different from far away.

People went far from the earth in spaceships.

They saw the whole earth from space.

This picture shows how the earth looks.

What shape is the earth?

▲ **Part of the earth from space**

Turn to page 240. Read I **Want to Be an Astronaut**. It tells you what astronauts do in space.

Pretend you are on a spaceship.

How would the earth look?

The land would look brown and green.

Blue oceans would cover most of the earth.

Many clouds would be around the earth.

How would the clouds look?

Lesson Review

1. How does the earth look from space?

2. What parts of the earth could you see from space?

Think! What things cannot be seen from space?

Explore
What covers most of the earth?

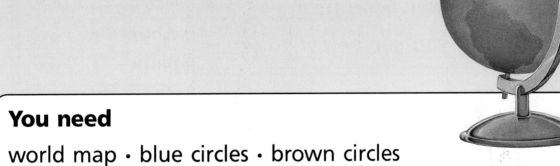

You need
world map · blue circles · brown circles

What to do
1. Look at the map.
2. Cover water with blue circles.
3. Cover land with brown circles.

4. Count the blue circles.
5. Count the brown circles.

What did you find out?
1. Which color did you use more?
2. What covers most of the earth?

2. How does the earth look from a jet?

Words to Know

mountain   river

plain   lake

Jets fly high above the earth.

But they fly lower than spaceships do.

This picture was taken from a jet.

What do you see?

▼ Earth from a jet

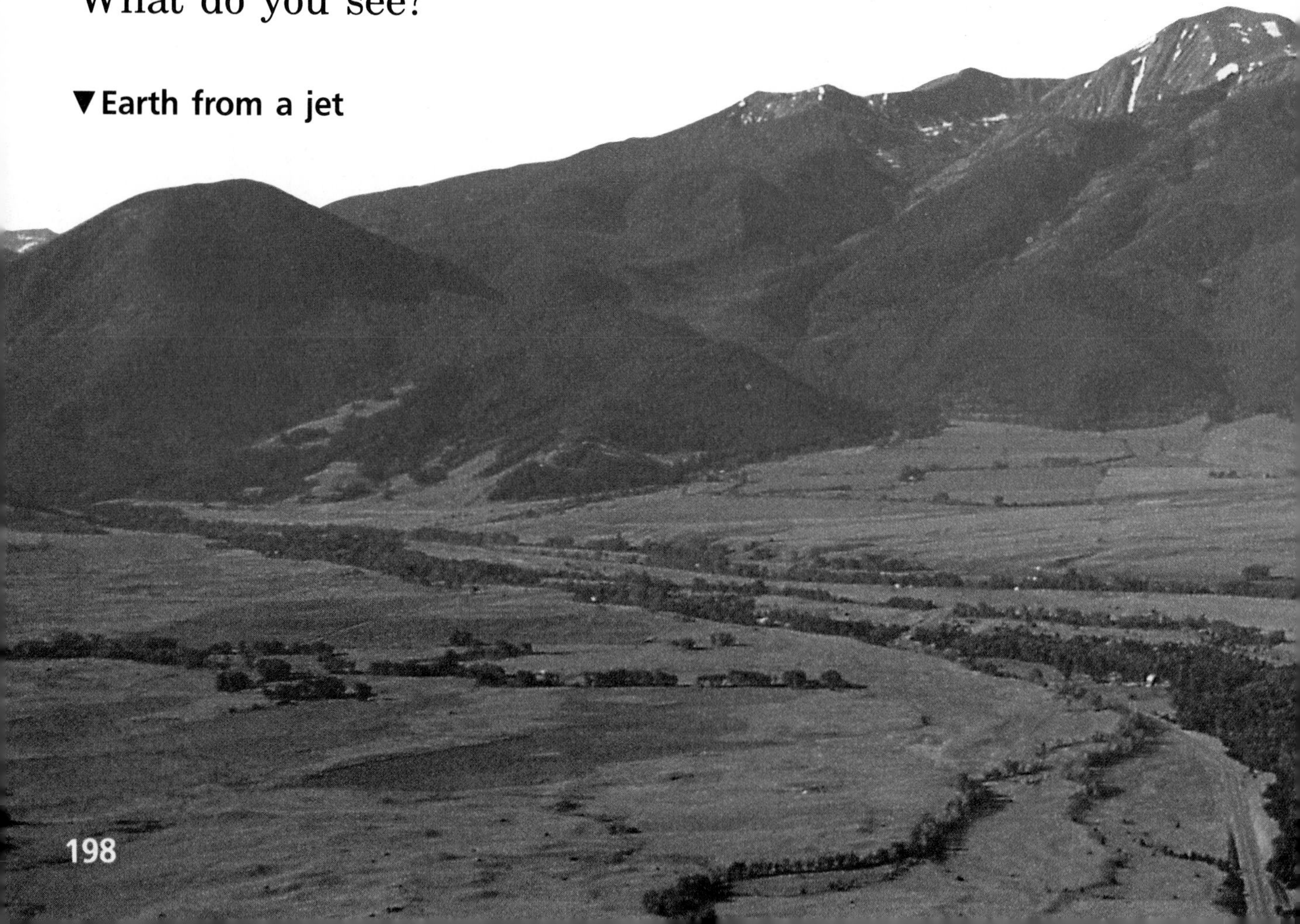

You might see land from a jet.

A **mountain** is a high point of land.

A **plain** is flat land.

Which picture shows a mountain?

Which picture shows a plain?

▲ Mountain

▲ Plain

◄Lake

▼Earth from a jet

◄River

You might see water from a jet.

A **river** is water that flows in a long, thin path.

It flows over the earth.

A **lake** is a body of water with land all around it.

Which picture shows a river?

Which picture shows a lake?

Suppose your jet flies over a city.

You might see things that people made.

You might see tall buildings.

You might see cars on the streets.

What other things might you see?

▲ City from a jet

Suppose your jet flies over farmland.

You might see plants growing in fields.

You might see houses and farm animals.

What else might you see?

▼ Farm

▲ Farmland

Lesson Review

1. What kinds of land and water can you see from a jet?

2. What things made by people can you see from a jet?

Think! Why do big things look small from a jet?

Skills

THINKING

Telling what you did and saw

You can find out about dirt in water.
You can tell what you did and what
you saw.

Practice

1. Put sand, dirt, and little stones
   in a jar of water.
   Cover the jar and shake it.
   Then put the jar on the table.
   Watch what happens.

2. Tell what you did to the jar.
   Tell what you saw in the jar.

Apply

Shake the jar again.

Pour what is in the jar through a screen.

Tell what you did.

Tell what you see on the screen.

3. How does the earth look from the ground?

Getting Started

Pretend you are in a park.

What might be on the ground?

Words to Know

rock   soil

You might see rocks on the ground.

A **rock** is a hard piece of the earth.

Rocks are different sizes, shapes, and colors.

How are these rocks alike?

How are they different?

204

Some rocks are all one color.

Other rocks are different colors.

Some rocks are smooth.

Other rocks are rough.

Tell about the rocks you see here.

▲ Rock arch

Soil is the top part of the earth.
Another word for soil is dirt.
Tiny bits of rock make up soil.
Soil has bits of dead plants in it.
It also has bits of dead animals.
Air and water are in soil too.

▼ Soil

There are different kinds of soil.
Some soil feels like powder.
Other soil feels like salt.

▲ Sandy soil

▲ Clay soil

Some soil has many bits of plants and animals.
Look at these kinds of soil.
What colors do you see?

▼ Topsoil

The earth has a lot of water.

You know water is in rivers and lakes.

This water is most often fresh water.

Where else do you see fresh water?

▼ Waterfall

▼ Pond

There is water in oceans too.
Ocean water is salty.

This large lake has salt water too.

Lesson Review

1. How are rocks alike and different?
2. Tell about two kinds of soil.
3. Where on the earth can you see water?

Think! What makes different kinds of soil different?

Problem Solving
Shapes in the Sand

This picture shows shapes in the sand.
The shapes were made by water.

How did water make these shapes?

Use a pan of sand.

Show how the shapes were made.

210

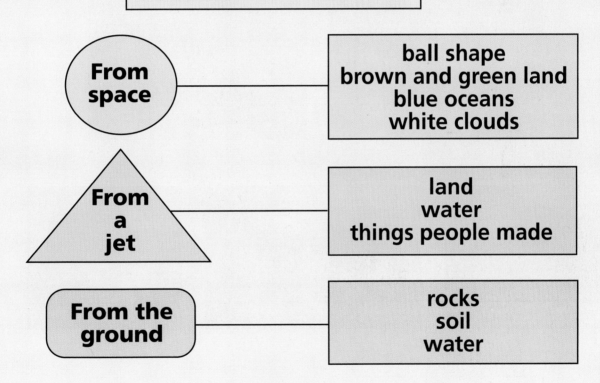

Chapter Connections

Draw a picture about one part of the word map.

Write a sentence to go with your picture.

LOOKING AT THE EARTH

From space

ball shape
brown and green land
blue oceans
white clouds

From a jet

land
water
things people made

From the ground

rocks
soil
water

Writing About Science • Classify

List things you see outside.

Underline the things you could see from a jet.

Circle the things you could see from space.

Science Words

Match each word with a picture.

earth   lake   mountain   plain
river   rock   soil

a

b

c

d

e

f

g

Science Ideas

1. How does the earth look from space?

2. How does the earth look from a jet?

3. How does the earth look from the ground?

Applying Science Ideas

What kind of soil is best for growing plants?
Tell why you think so.

Using Science Skills

Sprinkle water on dry soil.

Now pour water on dry soil.

Tell what you did and saw each time.

Chapter 8

Changes in the Weather

Rain, rain, go away.
Come again another day.

It is raining indoors!
This man is making a movie.
Where does the rain come from?

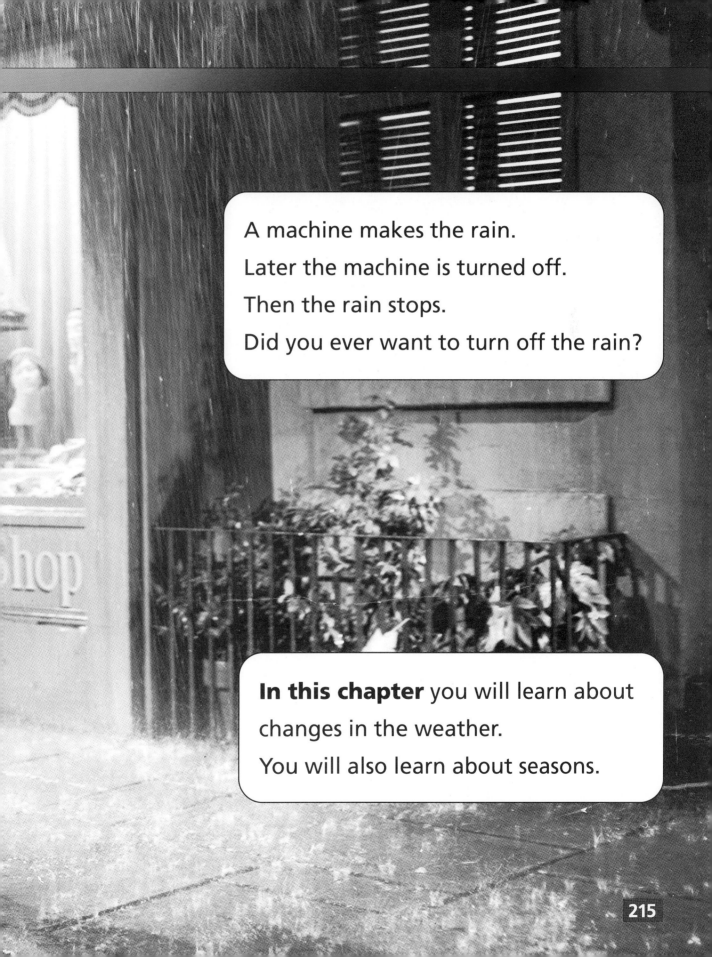

A machine makes the rain.

Later the machine is turned off.

Then the rain stops.

Did you ever want to turn off the rain?

In this chapter you will learn about changes in the weather.

You will also learn about seasons.

1. How does weather change?

Getting Started

Open a window.

Tell about the air outside.

Words to Know

weather

Weather is what the air outside is like.

The air around us is always changing.

So the weather is always changing.

Weather may change from warm to cool.

216

It may change from wet to dry.

Weather may change from sunny to cloudy.

It may change from calm to windy.

What weather change do these pictures show?

▲ Sun warming the earth

▲ Clouds blocking the sun

Why does weather change?

The sun makes weather change.

Sunlight warms the earth.

Then the earth warms the air.

Why is the air cool on a cloudy day?

Lesson Review

1. What are two ways the weather changes?

2. How does the sun make the weather change?

Think! Why is the air often cooler at night?

Problem Solving
Catch a Falling Raindrop

Rainy days are not all the same.

Sometimes the rain pours down hard.

Sometimes only a little rain falls.

How can you tell how much rain falls?

Think of a way to collect and measure rain.

What things will you need?

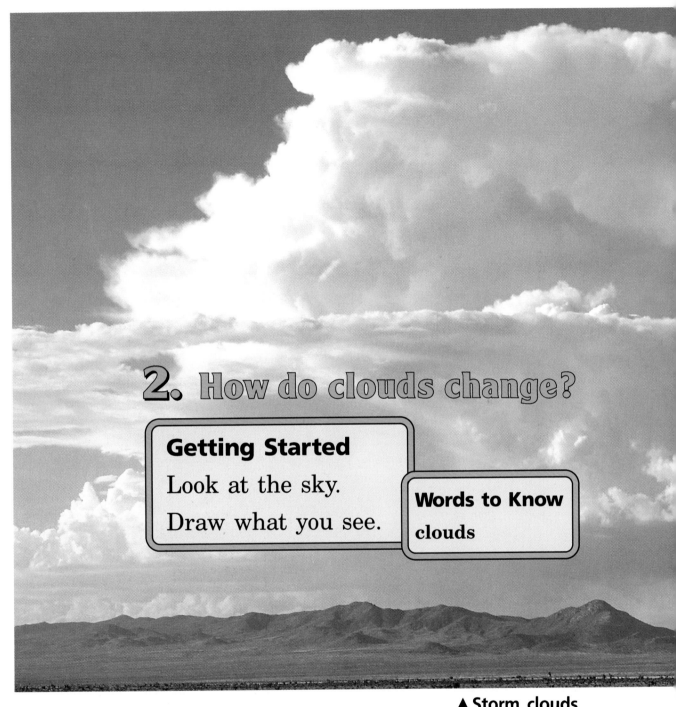

2. How do clouds change?

Getting Started

Look at the sky.
Draw what you see.

Words to Know

clouds

▲ Storm clouds

Clouds float in the air.

Clouds are made of tiny drops of water.

Many tiny drops make large drops.

▲ Rainstorm

The large drops are too heavy to float.
So the drops fall from the clouds.
They fall to the earth as rain.

You see light, fluffy clouds in sunny weather.
You see thick, gray clouds when it rains or snows.
What kinds of weather do these pictures show?

Lesson Review

1. When does it rain?

2. Tell about two kinds of clouds.

Think! Why is it helpful to know about clouds?

Explore

How do clouds move and change?

ACTIVITY

You need

plastic sheet · tape · red marker · blue marker

What to do

1. Look for a cloud.
2. Tape plastic on a window. **Be careful!** Do not lean against the window.
3. Trace around the cloud with a red marker.
4. Wait a few minutes.
5. Trace around the cloud with a blue marker.

What did you find out?

1. Did the cloud move?
2. Did it change shape?

3. How does weather change during the year?

Getting Started

Think about spring.

Tell why you like it.

Words to Know

season

▲ Woods in spring

Spring is a season.

A **season** is a time of the year.

There are four seasons in a year.

▼Mother deer with baby

Weather changes when a new season comes.

In spring the weather gets warm.

Plants begin to grow.

Many animals have their babies.

Tell about the living things in these pictures.

Summer weather can be very hot.

The sun shines for a long time each day.

Many plants grow flowers.

What are these young bears doing?

▼Black bear cubs

In fall the weather gets cool.

Some animals move to warmer places.

Some trees lose their leaves.

What is happening to these trees?

▲ Canada geese

▼ Trees in fall

Winter weather can be very cold.

Snow falls in some places.

Some animals sleep through the winter.

What is winter like where you live?

▼ Trees in winter

▲ Ground squirrel

Lesson Review

1. What is the weather like in each season?

2. How do living things change with the seasons?

Think! What changes do you make in each season?

OBSERVING

Skills
Seeing how things change

Clouds can block out the sun.

Later the clouds begin to move.

Then you can see the sun.

The sky has changed.

Practice

The pictures show the same animal in
summer and winter.

1. Tell how the rabbit changes.
2. Tell how other things in the second
   picture have changed.

Apply

This plant has changed.
Write all the changes you see.

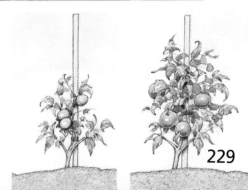

229

4. Why should you know about weather changes?

Getting Started

Think about the weather today.

What things could you do outside?

This woman studies the weather.

She uses a computer to help her.

She tells people how the weather might change.

Why do people want to know about weather changes?

These people are at the beach.

The weather is sunny and warm.

But the weather might change.

What weather changes might happen?

Sometimes weather changes quickly.

Look at these weather changes.

How can you tell that bad weather is coming?

Some bad weather can hurt you.

You can keep safe in bad weather.

A thunderstorm can bring lightning.

How do these people keep safe from lightning?

▼ **Thunderstorm with lightning**

Lesson Review

1. How can a weather change make you change plans?

2. How can you keep safe in bad weather?

Think! Tell how you feel in different kinds of weather.

ACTIVITY

Explore Together

How can you show weather changes?

You need

Planner | posterboard · markers · outdoor thermometer

What to do

Helper | **1.** Make a chart like the one shown.

Leader | **2.** Look outside.

Draw weather pictures on the chart.

Writer | **3.** Write words that tell about the weather.

All | **4.** Repeat steps **2** and **3** for 1 week.

	Wind	Sunny/Cloudy	Rain/Snow	Temperature
Monday		☁	🌧	18
Tuesday	🪁			
Wednesday				

What did you find out?

All | **1.** How did you show weather changes?

Reporter | **2.** Show the weather chart.

Tell how the weather changed.

234

Chapter Connections

Think about the word map.

Write a class story about it.

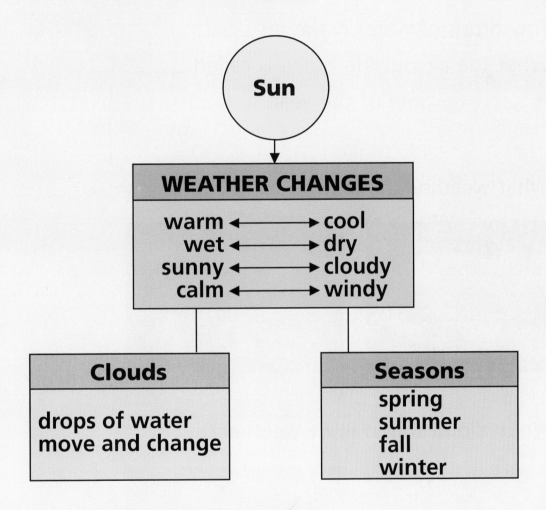

Writing About Science • Inform

Write the name of a season on paper.

Draw pictures about that season.

Science Words

Fill in each missing word.

clouds   season   weather

1. Tiny drops of water make up ____.

2. What the air outside is like is called ____.

3. A ____ is a time of the year.

Science Ideas

1. What weather changes do these pictures show?

a   b

2. Which cloud shows rainy weather?

a   b

3. What changes happen during this season?

4. How can you keep safe from lightning?

Applying Science Ideas

You are playing outside.

The sky gets dark and you hear thunder.

What should you do?

Using Science Skills

Look at these pictures.

Write all the changes you see.

Careers

Helicopter Pilot

Many people walk around the Grand Canyon.

But it looks different from above.

Rick Carrick is a **helicopter pilot**.

He flies people over the canyon.

Rick has always loved airplanes.

He learned to fly after high school.

Now Rick teaches other people to fly.

"I love being in the air," says Rick.

Connecting Science Ideas

1. The Grand Canyon is fun to fly over. What other places on the earth would you like to fly over?   **Careers; Chapter 7**

2. Some people work with telescopes. Why do they need to know what the weather will be?   **Chapter 6; Chapter 8**

3. You are flying in a jet. What can you tell about the weather on the ground?   **Chapter 7; Chapter 8**

4. You are on a spaceship. Why is there a shadow on part of the earth?

   Chapter 6; Chapter 7

Unit Project

Cut out pictures that show the earth.

Think about how far away the camera was.

Paste the pictures in order from near to far.

from

I Want to Be an Astronaut
Written and illustrated by Byron Barton

Would you like to be an astronaut?
Join these astronauts as they take a
trip to outer space!

I want to be an astronaut,
a member of the crew,
and fly on the shuttle
into outer space.

I want to be up there
on a space mission
and have ready-to-eat meals
and sleep in zero gravity.

I want to put on a space suit
and walk around in space
and help fix a satellite
and build a factory in orbit.

I want to be up there awhile
and then come back to Earth.

I just want to be an astronaut
and visit outer space.

Reader's Response

Would you like to be an astronaut when you grow up?
Tell why or why not.

I Want to Be an Astronaut

 Responding to Literature

1. Make a spaceship with things in your classroom. Tell where you would go in it.

2. Suppose you took a space trip. What would you do first when you came home? Ask friends what they would do.

3. You are an astronaut walking in space. Draw a picture of what you see. Write a name for your picture.

 Books to Enjoy

Saturn by Seymour Simon
Saturn is a planet that has rings and moons. This book has pictures of Saturn taken from spaceships.

Comets by Franklyn M. Branley
This book will answer your questions about comets.

HUMAN BODY

Growing Up

Which hand does this girl use
for throwing?
Some people use their right hand.
Others use their left hand.
People are different in many ways.
No one is just like you.

In this chapter you will learn that
each person is different.
You will also learn how people change
as they grow.

1. What makes you different from others?

Trees and flowers are alive.

Fish and mice are also alive.

People are alive too.

People are living things called **human beings**.

How are all human beings alike?

Human beings can do many things.

They can read books.

They can draw pictures.

Other living things cannot do these things.

What are these children doing?

You know human beings are alike in many ways.
But no two human beings are alike in all ways.
Fingerprints show that you are different.
Pictures show that you are different.
No one in the world is just like you.

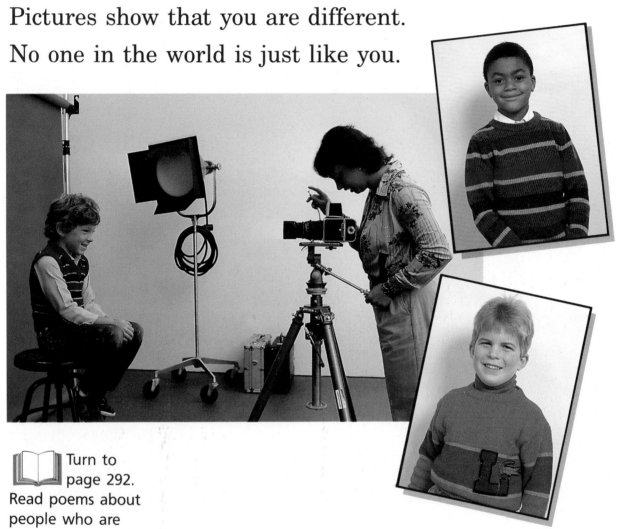

Turn to page 292. Read poems about people who are your age.

Lesson Review

1. How are people different from other living things?
2. How are you different from other people?

Think! How are you and your friends different?

ACTIVITY

Explore
Are all fingerprints the same?

Susan

You need

ink pad · white card · soap · water · hand lens

What to do

1. Press one finger on an ink pad.
2. Press that finger onto a card.
3. Wash your hands.
4. Look at your fingerprint with a hand lens.
5. Look at other fingerprints in your class.

What did you find out?

1. How is your fingerprint different from others?
2. Are any prints the same as yours?

253

2. What were you like as a baby?

Getting Started

Tell about a baby you know.

How does the baby look?

What things can the baby do?

Words to Know

infant

A baby grows inside its mother.

It grows for about nine months.

Then it is born.

A young baby is called an **infant**.

Babies are very small.

They have no teeth, and they sleep a lot.

Babies need a lot of care.

They cannot care for themselves.

How do you know when a baby needs care?

Babies use their senses to learn.

They touch things with their hands.

They put things into their mouth.

How are these babies using their senses?

Lesson Review

1. How do babies look and act?

2. How do babies use their senses to learn?

Think! What unsafe things could babies do?

Skills

Asking questions

How do people learn about things?

They ask questions.

Then they try to find answers.

Practice

Look at the picture.

What is happening in this picture?

What would you like to know about the baby?

Ask some questions.

Apply

What do you want to know about the animals?

Ask some questions.

257

3. What were you like as a young child?

Young children hear people talk.

Then they try to make the sounds.

This is how they learn to talk.

What words do young children learn first?

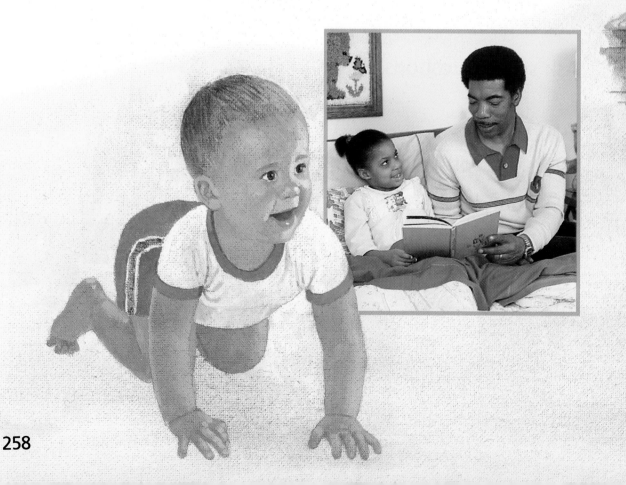

258

Young children like to move around.

First they crawl.

Then they learn to walk and run.

They learn to do many things with their hands.

They begin to care for themselves.

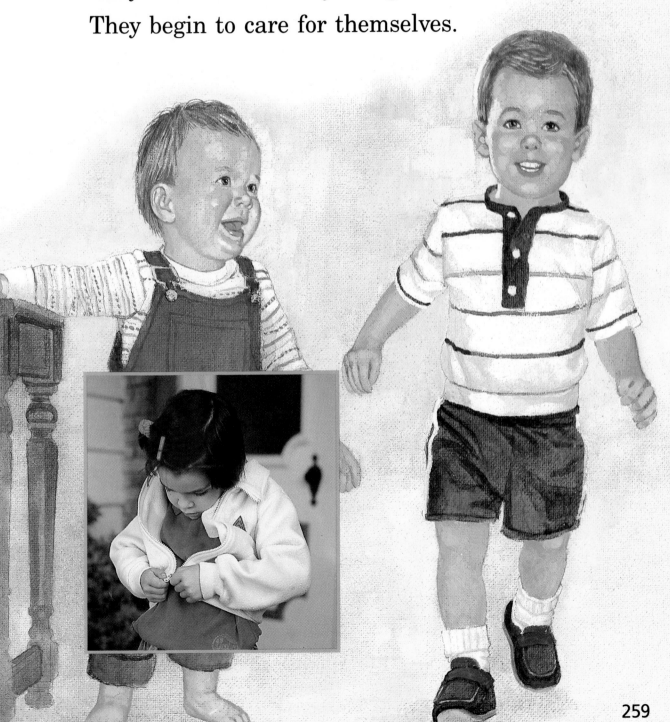

Young children grow in many ways.

They learn to do new things.

How is this child different from this baby?

Lesson Review

1. How do young children learn to talk?

2. What other things do young children learn to do?

Think! How are children different from each other?

ACTIVITY

Explore Together
What color eyes do you see?

You need

Planner | crayons · scissors · glue

What to do

All | **1.** Guess what color eyes most people have.

Writer | **2.** Write down your guess.

Leader | **3.** Look at the eyes of children in your group.

Helper | **4.** Draw one eye for each child.
Show the color of the eye.

Leader | **5.** Cut out each eye.

Helper | **6.** Paste each eye on a class chart.

	brown	blue	black	green	gray
3	eye				
2	eye	eye			
1	eye	eye		eye	

What did you find out?

All | **1.** What color eyes were in your group?

Reporter | **2.** What color are most eyes in your class?

261

4. How are you changing?

Getting Started

Look at an old picture of yourself.
Now look at a new picture.
How have you changed?

Words to Know

adult

You cannot see yourself grow.

But you change every day.

Every day you grow new skin, hair, and nails.

Sometimes a baby tooth falls out.

A new, bigger tooth grows in its place.

Think how small you used to be.

Your clothes and shoes were very small.

They would not fit you now.

How can you tell that you are changing?

Someday you will be a teenager.

Most teenagers grow very fast.

Young children are smaller than their parents.

Teenagers may be as big as their parents.

◀Young child

Teenager▶

Someday you will be an adult.

An **adult** is a fully grown person.

Adults do not grow taller.

But they change in other ways.

How do adults change as they grow older?[3]

Adults

Lesson Review

1. What happens to your teeth as you grow?

2. How will you change as you grow up?

Think! What is good about growing older?

Problem Solving
Who Am I?

You change as you grow.

The way you look changes.

The things you play with change.

The things you like to do change.

What are you like now?

Do you think you will remember next year?

Find things that show what you are like now.

Think of a way to save them.

Then you can look at them next year.

266

Chapter Connections

Copy the four shapes on pieces of paper.

Mix them up.

Try to put them back in the right order.

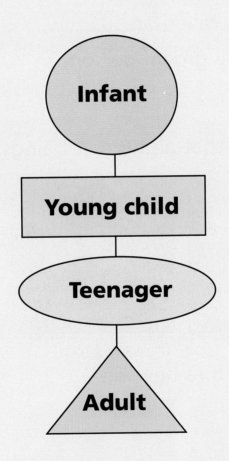

Writing About Science • Narrate

Write about something you just learned to do.

Draw a picture to go with your writing.

Science Words

Fill in each missing word.

adult   human beings   infant

1. People are called ____.

2. A young baby is called an ____.

3. An ____ is a fully grown person.

Science Ideas

1. Name two ways that all human beings are different.

2. What care do babies need?

3. What things do young children learn to do?

4. How are you changing?

Applying Science Ideas

People are different from each other.
Why are these differences good?

Using Science Skills

We do not always
know why babies cry.
Write a question
about this baby.

10
Staying Healthy

Who uses dust for a bath?

Elephants do!

It is dry where they live.

Sometimes they take a bath using dust.

They suck up dust in their trunk.
Then they spray it on their skin.
The dust gets rid of bugs.
How do you keep clean?

In this chapter you will learn
how to stay healthy.
You will find out who helps you
stay well.

1. How can you stay healthy?

Getting Started

List some foods you like.

Which foods are good for you?

Words to Know

healthy

exercise

rest

Healthy means being well.

Some foods help you stay healthy.

Meat, fish, and milk are healthful foods.

Fruits, vegetables, and breads are good foods too.

Foods with a lot of fat are not good for you.

Exercise means moving your body.

Exercise helps you stay healthy.

You should exercise each day.

These children are playing outdoors.

Playing outdoors is good exercise.

How do you exercise each day?

To **rest** means to stop moving.

You rest when you sit still or sleep.

Each day your body needs rest.

Rest helps you stay healthy.

How do you feel without enough rest?

Lesson Review

1. Name four foods that are good for you.

2. What other things help you stay healthy?

Think! What are some ways you rest?

Explore Together

Which snacks have a lot of fat?

You need

brown paper squares ·
oil · dropper · snacks

What to do

Writer **1.** Write each food name on a paper square.

Helper **2.** Put a drop of oil on one paper square.
Oil is one kind of fat.

Leader **3.** Rub each snack on a paper square.
Be careful! Do not eat these snacks.

All **4.** Hold each paper square up to the light.

What did you find out?

All **1.** How did the oil change the paper?

All **2.** How did each snack change the paper?

Reporter **3.** Which snacks have a lot of fat?

275

2. Why should you keep clean?

Getting Started

Have you ever been sick?

How did you feel?

Words to Know

sick

germs

heal

Sick means not healthy.

Sometimes germs make you sick.

Germs are tiny living things.

They are too small to see.

Keeping clean helps to get rid of germs.

How are these people keeping clean?

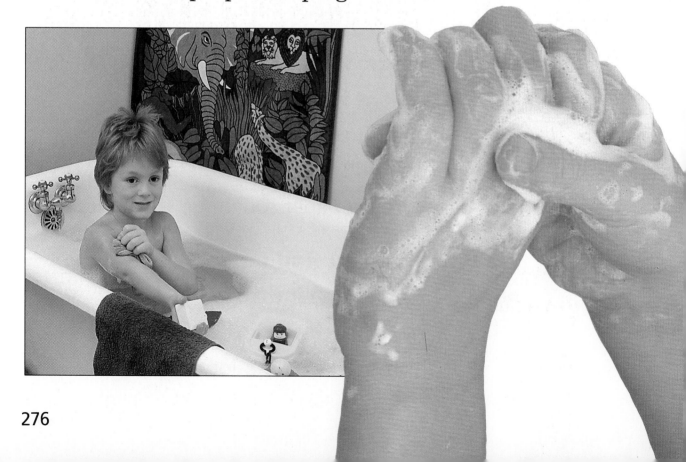

276

This girl has a cold.

One sneeze can spread many germs.

The germs can reach other people.

Then other people may catch a cold too.

How can the girl stop spreading germs?

Have you ever had a cut?

Soon the cut will be gone.

Your body will heal the cut.

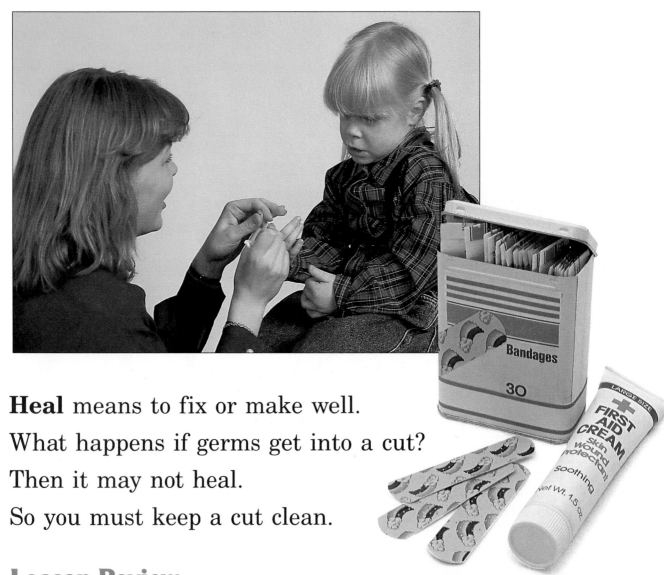

Heal means to fix or make well.

What happens if germs get into a cut?

Then it may not heal.

So you must keep a cut clean.

Lesson Review

1. How can germs harm you?

2. How can staying clean keep you healthy?

Think! What can you do if someone is spreading germs?

THINKING

Skills

Telling what happens next

You jump up.

Then you drop back down.

You do one thing.

Then another thing happens.

Practice

1. Pretend you cut your knee.

Tell what might happen then.

2. Pretend you get a new pet.

Tell what might happen then.

Apply

Pretend you do not wear a raincoat one day.

Later in the day it begins to rain.

Tell what might happen then.

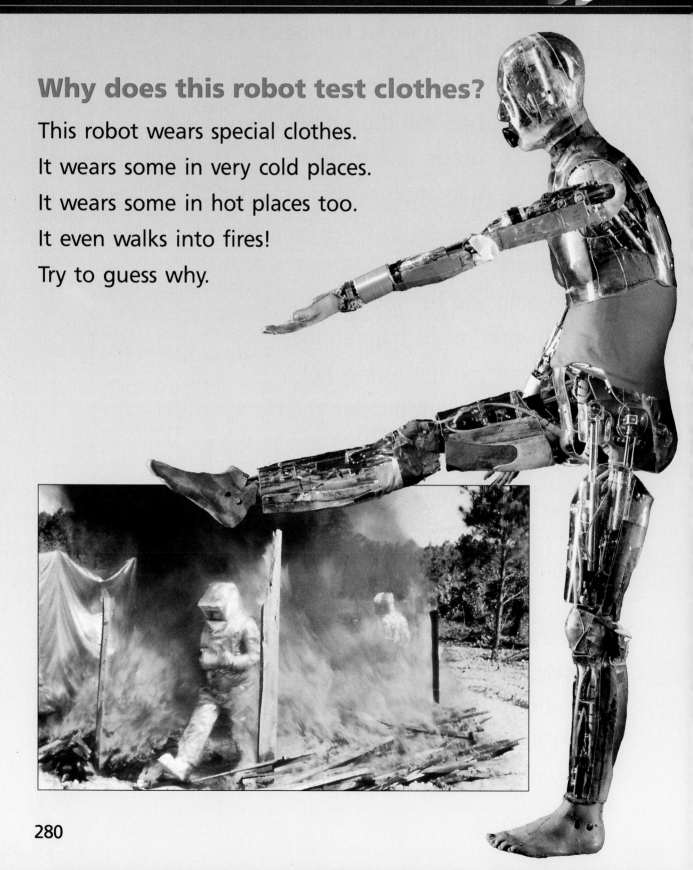

Why does this robot test clothes?

This robot wears special clothes.

It wears some in very cold places.

It wears some in hot places too.

It even walks into fires!

Try to guess why.

STS

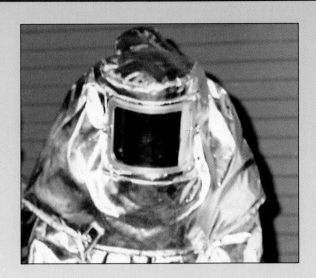

The robot is testing the clothes.

It tests jackets for people who fight fires.

It tests clothes for other workers too.

Then people know the clothes are safe.

Thinking about it

1. Why is this robot used to test clothes?

2. What other ways can robots help people?

Using what you learned

Some jobs put people in danger.

Talk to someone who has that kind of job.

What does that person wear for safety?

Tell the class what you learned.

3. Who helps you stay healthy?

Getting Started

Did you ever get sick at school?

Who helped you?

Words to Know

doctors

checkup

dentists

Sometimes you may go to a doctor.

Doctors can help sick people.

A doctor can give you a shot.

The shot can make you well.

Doctors also help people who are hurt.

How has a doctor helped you?

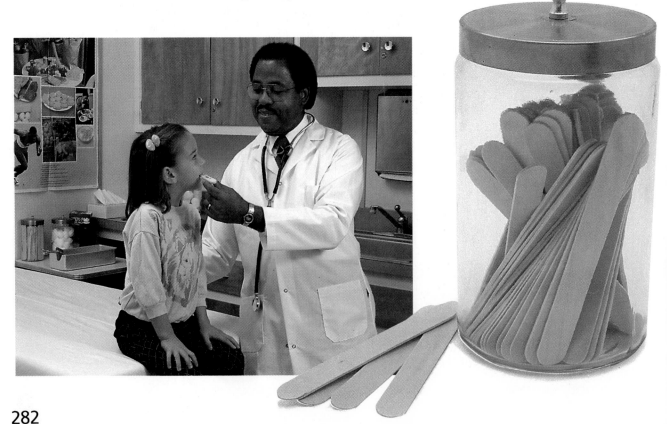

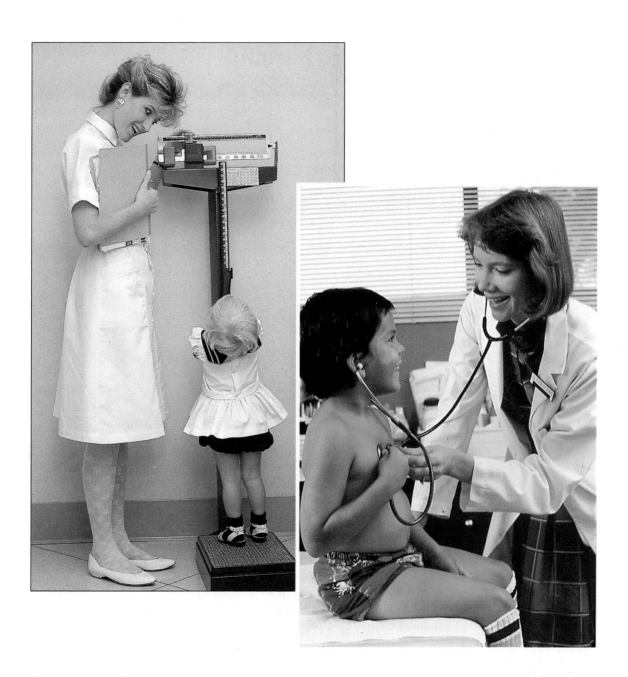

Doctors help people stay healthy too.

This boy is not sick.

The doctor is checking his whole body.

This is called a **checkup**.

What does the doctor look for?

Some sicknesses are very harmful.

How can you keep from getting a harmful sickness?

A doctor can give you a shot.

You get the shot when you are healthy.

The shot keeps you from getting sick.

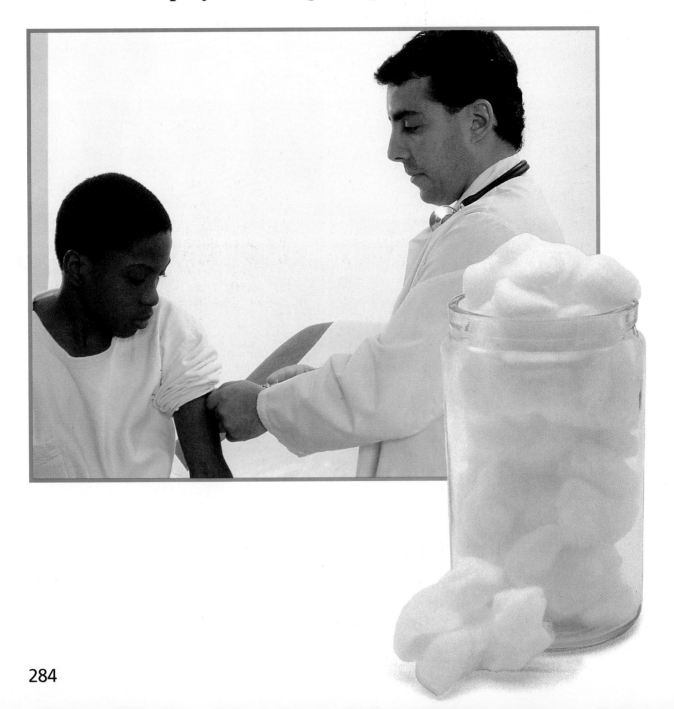

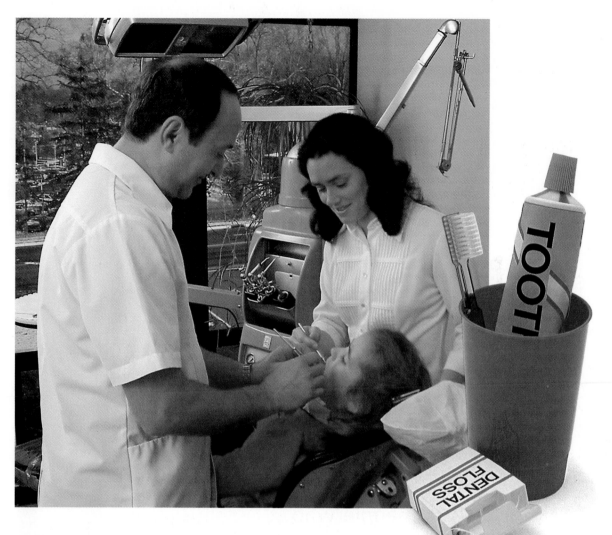

Dentists take care of your teeth.
This girl is having a dental checkup.
The dentist looks at her teeth and gums.
How should you take care of your teeth at home?

Lesson Review

1. Who helps you stay healthy?
2. Name two things that help keep you healthy.

Think! Would you like to be a doctor? Why?

Explore

How do people at school keep you healthy?

You need

paper · pencil

What to do

1. Many people work in your school. They do things to keep you healthy. Make a list of these people.
2. Choose two people who help you stay healthy.
3. Ask them what they do on their jobs. Write down what they say.

What did you find out?

1. How do these people help you stay healthy?
2. Suppose these people did not do their jobs. What would happen?

286

Chapter Connections

Cover one part of this word map.

Ask a classmate to guess what is missing.

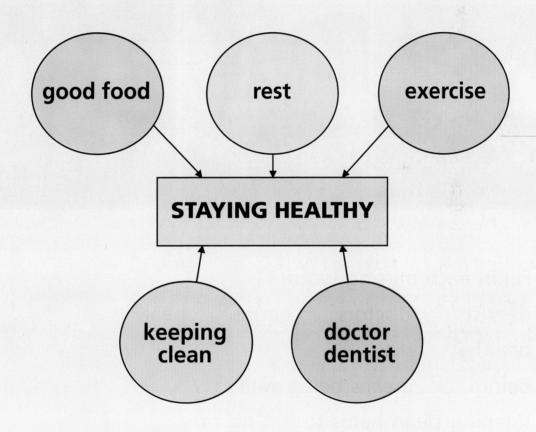

good food

rest

exercise

STAYING HEALTHY

keeping clean

doctor dentist

Writing About Science • Describe

Make a web with <u>Staying Healthy</u> in the middle.

Draw things you do to stay healthy.

Science Words

A. Match each word with a picture.

checkup   exercise   rest

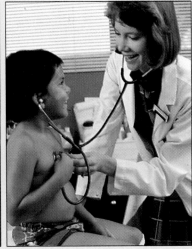

a   b   c

B. Fill in each missing word.

dentists   doctors   germs   heal

healthy   sick

1. Being ____ means being well.

2. Keeping clean helps to get rid of ____.

3. Sick people get help from ____.

4. Being ____ means not being healthy.

5. Your body can often ____ itself.

6. Teeth are checked by ____.

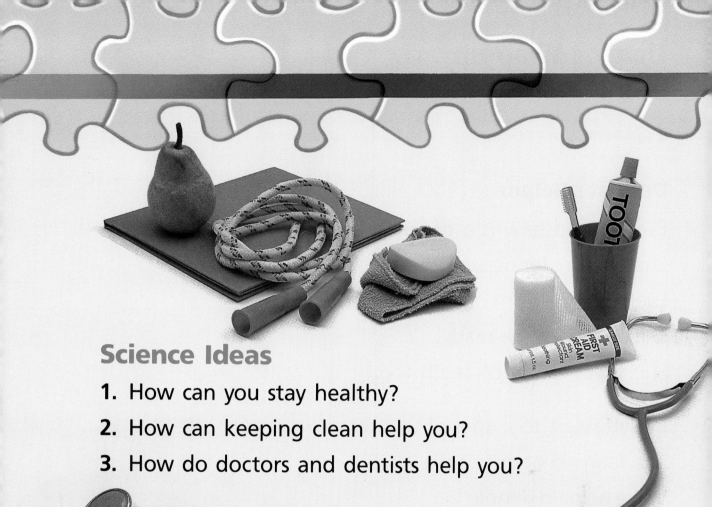

Science Ideas

1. How can you stay healthy?

2. How can keeping clean help you?

3. How do doctors and dentists help you?

Applying Science Ideas

People use robots to test clothing.

How else could people use robots?

Using Science Skills

Suppose you take a nap after lunch.

Tell how you might feel after your nap.

Careers

Dentist's Helper

Evelyn Bradshaw is a **dentist's helper**.

She lives in Tennessee.

Evelyn works right next to the **dentist.**

She gets the tools ready.

She takes X-rays of teeth too.

Evelyn went to a special school.

She learned about teeth.

"I like helping people,"

Evelyn says.

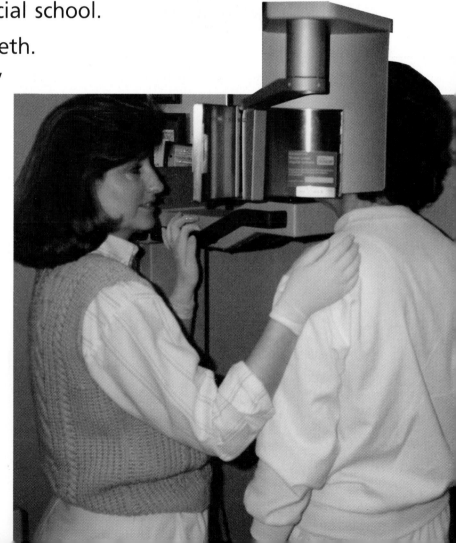

Connecting Science Ideas

1. You read about a dentist's helper.

What work might a doctor's helper do?

Careers; Chapter 10

2. How do infants exercise?

How do adults exercise?

Chapter 9; Chapter 10

3. What can a young child

do to stay healthy?

Chapter 9; Chapter 10

4. You read about a robot that tests clothes.

Why should infants' clothes be tested?

Chapter 9; Chapter 10

Calculator Connection

Guess how many times your classmates can jump.

Have your teacher time 1 minute.

Use a calculator to find the total jumps.

Every day you grow and change.
Read these poems about growing up.

All My Hats

All my hats
are hats he wore.
What a bore.

All my pants
are pants he ripped.
What a gyp.

All my books
are books he read.
What a head.

All my fights
are fights he fought.
What a thought.

All my steps
are steps he tried.
What a guide.

All my teachers
call me by my brother's name.
What a shame.

Richard J. Margolis

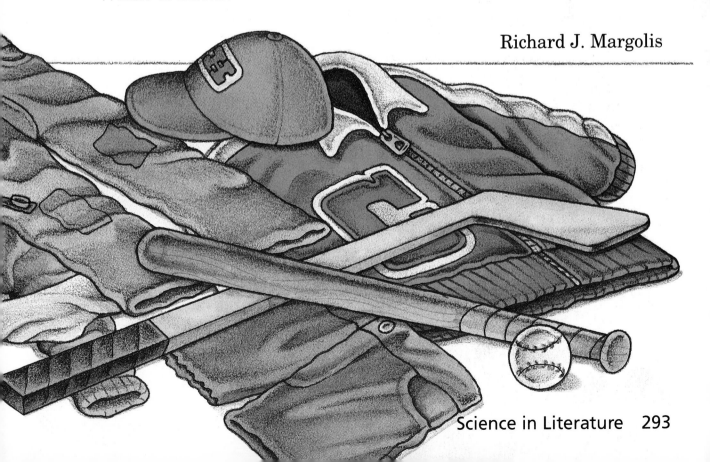

TWO WHEELS

I told you I won't. It's too hard.
I told you I can't. It's too hard.
Didn't I tell you?

My feet, they won't reach.
My hands, they won't steer.
It's too hard.

Watch out—I'm tipping.
Don't let go—I'm falling.
Please: I give up.

Not so fast, not so fast.
I don't like this.
Stop stop stop stop.

Hey, I can't stop.
Hey, I'm riding, I'm riding.
Hey hey hey hey hey.

Did you see me?
What did I tell you?
It was easy.

Richard J. Margolis

295

What We Are Going To Be

Everybody asks us
what are we going to be.

The captain of a ship,
or a doctor, or a sculptor?
A dentist, an architect,
a writer, or a painter?

All the different kinds of work
have certain charms all their own.
Choosing is not an easy task—
there are so many we can choose from!

To fly through space,
or to heal sick animals?
To plow the land,
or to draw and paint murals?

There is a promise that is inside
each future that we might employ.
There is no work which is too hard
if it is done with joy.

And what is most important
is that we know and see:
nothing can stand in the way
of what we really want to be!

Alma Flor

translated by Rose Zubizarreta

Reader's Response

It is fun to learn new things.
What have you learned this year?

Poems

📖 Responding to Literature

1. Read the poem "All My Hats" again.
   Draw a picture of your favorite part.
   Write a sentence about your picture.

2. Have you ever said, "It's too hard!
   I give up!"
   What is the hardest thing you ever did?

3. When you grow up, what do you want
   to be?
   Ask some friends what they want to be.

📖 Books to Enjoy

Eat Up, Gemma by Sarah Hayes
An older brother gets his baby sister to eat
her food.

Leo the Late Bloomer by Robert Kraus
Leo does things when he is ready.
Leo's parents think he is not growing up
fast enough.

Glossary

A

adult   An adult is a fully grown person. An adult does not grow taller. page 265

B

body parts   Body parts of animals help the animals live. A beak is a body part of a bird. page 56

C

checkup   A check by a doctor of your whole body. page 283

clouds   Clouds are tiny drops of water. They float in the air. Rain falls from some clouds. page 220

cone   A cone is a part of some plants. Seeds form in cones. page 86

D

daytime   Daytime is the light part of a day. You go to school in the daytime. page 184

dentist   A dentist takes care of your teeth. The dentist checks your teeth and gums. page 285

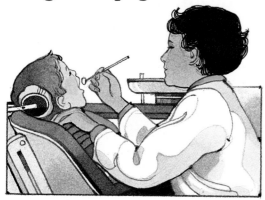

desert   A desert is a dry place on the earth. Cactus plants live in deserts. page 92

doctor   A doctor helps sick people. Doctors help people stay healthy too. page 282

E
earth   We live on the earth. The earth is round like a ball. page 194

exercise   Exercise is moving your body. Playing outdoors is good exercise. page 273

F
flower   A flower is a part of some plants. Seeds form in flowers. page 84

force A force is a push or a pull. A large force is needed to move a heavy rock. page 140

forest A forest is a shady, wet place where trees grow. Ferns and mosses grow in a forest. page 90

full moon The full moon looks like a circle. On some nights there is a full moon. page 175

germs Germs are tiny living things. They can make you sick. Germs are too small to be seen. page 276

gravity Gravity is a force. It pulls things to the earth. Gravity makes a ball fall down. page 146

heal Heal means to fix or make well. Your body will heal a cut. page 278

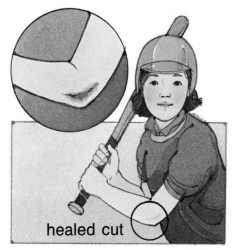

healed cut

healthy   Healthy means being well. Some foods help to keep you healthy. page 272

human beings   Human beings are people. You are a human being. page 250

I

infant   An infant is a young baby. An infant needs a lot of care. page 254

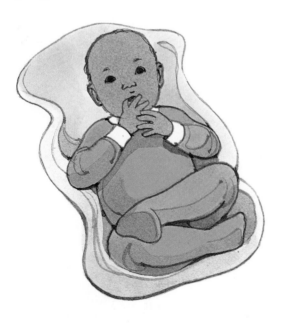

L

lake   A lake is a body of water with land all around it. People swim in some lakes. page 200

leaves   Leaves are parts of a plant. They make food. Some plants have flat leaves. page 82

length   Length is how long something is. You can find out the length of a fish. page 121

lever A lever is a machine. A lever makes it easier to lift things. A seesaw is a lever. page 153

living thing A living thing is alive. Living things move, need food, and grow. page 32

M

machine A machine makes work easier. Machines help people push, pull, and lift. page 150

measure To measure is to find out how long something is, how heavy something is, or how much something holds. page 121

mountain A mountain is a high point of land. Some people climb mountains. page 199

move To move is to go from place to place. Animals move from place to place. page 36

N

night Night is the dark part of a day. You sleep at night. page 184

P

plain A plain is flat land. You can see far on a plain. page 199

pond A pond is a body of still water. Cattails grow near ponds. page 94

R

ramp A ramp is a machine. A ramp makes it easier to lift things. A mover uses a ramp to lift things into a truck. page 152

rest To rest is to stop moving. You rest when you sit still or sleep. page 274

river A river is a body of water. It flows in a long, thin path. Rivers flow over the earth. page 200

rock　A rock is a hard piece of the earth. Rocks are different sizes, shapes, and colors. page 204

root　A root is a plant part. Roots take in water. page 88

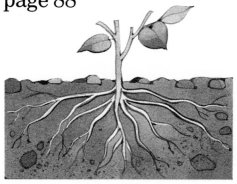

S

scale　A scale measures how heavy something is. The scale shows how heavy the cat is.　page 125

season　A season is a time of year. Spring, summer, fall, and winter are the seasons.　page 224

seed　A seed is part of a plant. It grows into a new plant. A sunflower has seeds in the center of the flower.　page 85

senses　People use their senses to help them learn about things. Seeing, hearing, smelling, tasting, and touching are the senses.　page 116

shelter　A shelter is a safe place to live. A hole in the ground is shelter for a badger.　page 42

sick   Sick is not being healthy. A cold makes you sick. page 276

soil   Soil is the top part of the earth. Another word for soil is dirt. page 206

star   A star is a body in space. Stars give off light as the sun does. page 178

stem   A stem is a plant part. Water and food move through stems. Some stems are hard. page 87

sunrise   Sunrise is the time when the sun comes up in the east. The sky gets light at sunrise. page 171

sunset   Sunset is the time when the sun sets in the west. The sky gets dark at sunset. page 171

T

texture   Texture is how something feels. Rough and smooth are textures. page 118

W

weather   Weather is
what the air outside is like.
Weather may change from
warm to cool.   page 216

weight   Weight is how
heavy something is. The
doctor needs to know your
weight.   page 125

wheel   A wheel is one
kind of machine. A bicycle
has wheels.   page 151

Index

Credits

m. Tom Kitchin/TOM STACK & ASSOCIATES; *b.* Dan DeWilde for SB&G. 99: Dan DeWilde for SB&G. 102: *l.* P. Kresan/H. Armstrong Roberts; *m.* W. Geiersperger/The Stock Market; *r.* Milton Rand/TOM STACK & ASSOCIATES. 103: *t.l.* © Noble Proctor/Photo Researchers, Inc. *t.m.* D. Muench/H. Armstrong Roberts; *t.r.* E.R. Degginger/Color-Pic, Inc. 104: Courtesy of Michigan State University. 105: IMAGERY.

Unit 2 opener   113: T.J. Florian/Rainbow.

Chapter 4   114–115: Richard Faverty/Beckett Studios. 116: Stuart M. Williams/M.L. Dembinsky. 117: *t.r.* E.R. Degginger/Color-Pic, Inc.; *m.m.* Joe S. Sroka/M.L. Dembinsky. 118: *t.l.* Stuart M. Williams/M.L. Dembinsky; *b.r.* © Walter Chandoha 1991. 119: Dan DeWilde for SB&G. 120–121: Courtesy of Lego Systems, Inc. 123: *t.* Light Mechanics for SB&G; *b.* Ken O'Donoghue for SB&G. 124–125: Courtesy of Animal Hospital, Clinton-Perryville, by SB&G. 126: *t.l.* Courtesy of U.S. Postal Service; *t.r.* Courtesy of Superfoodtown, Cedar Knolls, NJ. 134: *m.* E.R. Degginger/Color-Pic, Inc.; *b.* Courtesy of Lego Systems, Inc.

Chapter 5:   136–137: Mathew Smith. 136: *b.l.* Bill Kontzias. 137: *m.m.* Bill Ballenberg/*Life Magazine* © Time, Inc. 140: Len Berger/Berg & Associates. 143: Light Mechanics for SB&G. 144: Adaptive Machine Technologies, Inc. 145: Runk/Schoenberger/Grant Heilman Photography. 150: *t.* Jackie Foryst/Bruce Coleman. 150: *b.l.* Kirk Schlea/Berg & Associates. 150: *b.r.* Sandy Roessler/The Stock Market. 151: David Stone/Berg & Associates. 152: *b.* Margaret C. Berg/Berg & Associates. 153: J. Gerard Smith for SB&G. 156: Margaret Berg/Berg & Associates. 158: Courtesy of Altom Takeyosu/Kenner Products. 159: Stephen J. Kraseman/Peter Arnold, Inc.

Unit 3 opener   167: Galen Rowell/Peter Arnold, Inc.

Chapter 6   168–169: © Jerry Schad/Photo Researchers, Inc. 169: *t.r.* Steve Elmore/TOM STACK & ASSOCIATES. 170: *m.l.* Comstock; *b.r.* Comstock. 171: E.R. Degginger/Color-Pic, Inc. 173: Stephen G. Maka. 174–175: *t.* © John Bova/Photo Researchers, Inc. 175: *b.* Bruce W. Heinemann/The Stock Market. 176: *t.r.* NASA/Stock, Boston; *m.l.* © Hale Observatories/Science Source/Photo Researchers, Inc. 178: Zefa U.K./H. Armstrong Roberts. 179: © Jerry Schad/Photo Researchers, Inc. 180: Richard D. Wood/Taurus Photos, Inc. 182–183: Tom Ives. 184: *t.l.* Brownie Harris/The Stock Market. 184–185: *b.m.* Allen Russell/Profiles West. 185: *t.m.* Dan DeWilde for SB&G. 190: *t.* © 1988 John Bova/Photo Researchers, Inc.; *m.* Zefa U.K./H. Armstrong Roberts. 191: *t.* © 1988 John Bova/Photo Researchers, Inc.

Chapter 7   192–193: © 1991 A. Griffiths Belt/Woodfin Camp & Associates. 192: *m.* Larry Lefever/Grant Heilman Photography. 194: M. Bob Woodward/The Stock Market. 195: David G. Johnson/Unicorn Stock Photos. 196: NASA. 197: Dan DeWilde for SB&G. 198: Kenneth & Talita Paolini/Profiles West. 199: *t.m.* W. Perry Conway/TOM STACK & ASSOCIATES; *b.r.* Stan Osolinski/The Stock Market. 200: *t.* Tim Haske/Profiles West; *m.* Animals Animals/Brian Milne/Earth Scenes; *b.* Brian Parker/TOM STACK & ASSOCIATES. 201: Bill Nation/Picture Group 1986. 202: *t.m.* Andris Apse/Bruce Coleman; *t.r.* Sharon Cummings/M.L. Dembinsky. 203: Light Mechanics for SB&G. 204–205: Breck P. Kent for SB&G. 205: *b.m.* Stan Osolinski/M.L. Dembinsky. 208: *b.* Stan Osolinski/M.L. Dembinsky; *t.r.* Lois Moulton/f-Stop Pictures. 209: *t.* Matt Lindsay/Berg & Associates; *m.l.* E.R. Degginger/Color-Pic, Inc. 210: Glen Short, 1980/Bruce Coleman. 212: *t.l.* W. Perry Conway/TOM STACK & ASSOCIATES; *t.r.* Bob Woodward/The Stock Market; *m.l.* Brian Parker/TOM STACK & ASSOCIATES; *m.m.* Tim Haske/Profiles West; *m.r.* NASA; *b.l.* Breck P. Kent for SB&G. 213: *t.* David G. Johnson/Unicorn Stock Photo; *m.* Bill Nation/Picture Group.

Chapter 8   214–215: Springer/The Bettmann Archive. 219: Dan DeWilde for SB&G. 220: Phil Degginger/Color-Pic, Inc. 221: Phil Degginger/Color-Pic, Inc. 222: *t.m.* Animals Animals/Phillip Hart/Earth Scenes; *b.* Bart Barlow/Envisions. 224: *t.* Robert P. Carr/Bruce Coleman; *m.* M.L. Dembinsky. 225: *t.* Robert P. Carr/Bruce Coleman; *m.* Animals Animals/Leonard Lee Rue III. 226–227: Sharon Cummings/M.L. Dembinsky. 226: *b.* Ted Reuther/M.L. Dembinsky. 227: *t.* Animals Animals/Ray Richardson; *b.* Ken Straiton/The Stock Market. 228: *l.* David Madison/Bruce Coleman; *r.* Jeff Foott/Bruce Coleman. 229: *l.* Len Lee Rue III/Stock, Boston. 229: *r.* Tom Walker/Stock, Boston. 230: Brownie Harris/The Stock Market. 231–232: *t.m.* © Charles Mayer/Science Source/Photo Researchers, Inc. 231: *t.* Warren Faubel/After Image. 232: *t.* Steve Elmore/The Stock Market; *b.* Tom McCarthy/Unicorn Stock Photos. 233: Arthur Roslund/f-Stop Pictures. 236: *b.l.* Phillip Hart/Earth Scenes; *b.r.* Bart Barlow/Envisions. 237: *b.m.* © Charlie Ott/Photo Researchers, Inc.; *b.m.* Ken Straiton/The Stock Market; *b.r.* Stan Osolinski/M.L. Dembinsky. 238: Courtesy of Rick Carrick.

Unit 4 opener   247: David Madison 1990.

Chapter 9   248–249: Yoav Levy. 249: *t.* Ken Karp. 256: *t.l.* Laura Dwight/Peter Arnold, Inc. 257: *m.r.* Ken Lax for SB&G; *b.r.* Animals Animals/Zig Leszczynski. 258: *b.r.* Michael Heron for SB&G. 259: Elizabeth Zuckerman/Photo Edit. 260: Dan DeWilde for SB&G. 263: © Lawrence Migdale/Photo Researchers, Inc. 264: Courtesy of The Henry Family, NJ. 265: *t.r.* M. Richards/Photo Edit; *m.m.* FourByFive, Inc. 269: *t.l.* Michael Heron for SB&G. 269: *t.r.* Elizabeth Zuckerman/Photo Edit.

Chapter 10   270–271: © Sven-Olof Lindblad/Photo Researchers, Inc. 273: Macdonald Photography/Envisions. 278: *t.m.* Erika Stone. 279: Light Mechanics for SB&G. 280–281: NASA/Science Source Photo Researchers. 280: *m.r.* Battelle Pacific Northwest Laboratories. 281: J. Robertson/U.S. Army Photograph. 283: *t.l.* T. Barber/

Custom Medical Stock Photo. 283: *t.r.* T. Fuller/Custom Medical Stock Photo. 284: Custom Medical Stock Photo. 288: *m.m.* T. Fuller/Custom Medical Stock Photo. 288: *m.r.* Macdonald Photography/Envisions. 290: Courtesy of Evelyn Bradshaw.

ACKNOWLEDGMENTS

Grateful acknowledgment is made to the following publishers, authors, and agents for their permission to reprint copyrighted material. Any adaptations are noted in the individual acknowledgments and are made with the full knowledge and approval of the authors or their representatives. Every effort has been made to locate all copyright proprietors; any errors or omissions in copyright notices are inadvertent and will be corrected in future printings as they are discovered.

pp. 106–112: *Deer at the Brook* by Jim Arnosky. Text and illustrations Copyright © 1986 by Jim Arnosky. By permission of Lothrop, Lee & Shepard Books (A Division of William Morrow & Co.) and of Susan Schulman Literary Agency, Inc.

pp. 160–166: From *Wheel Away!* by Dayle Ann Dodds. Text Copyright © 1989 by Dayle Ann Dodds, illustrations copyright © 1989 by Thacher Hurd. Reprinted by permission of Harper & Row, Publishers, Inc., and of Curtis Brown, Ltd.

pp. 240–246: *I Want to Be an Astronaut* by Byron Barton (Crowell). Copyright © 1988 by Byron Barton. Reprinted by permission of Harper & Row, Publishers, Inc.

pp. 292–293: "All My Hats" from *Secrets of a Small Brother* by Richard J. Margolis. Text Copyright © 1984 by Richard J. Margolis. Reprinted with permission of Macmillan Publishing Company.

pp. 294–295: "Two Wheels" from *Secrets of a Small Brother* by Richard J. Margolis. Text Copyright © 1984 by Richard J. Margolis. Reprinted with permission of Macmillan Publishing Company.

pp. 296–297: "What We Are Going to Be," translation by Rose Zubizarreta of the poem "Lo que vamos a ser" by Alma Flor Ada. Translated and reprinted by permission of Addison-Wesley Publishing Company, Inc.